USS Los Angeles (CA-135) Cold War Sentinel

CW00953362

by Harvey M. Beigel

LIBRARY OF CONGRESS
CATALOG CARD NUMBER 99–80005

ISBN 1-57510-067-3

First Printing: December 1999
Front cover is one of Arthur Beaumont's wartime paintings of the *USS Los Angeles*,
courtesy of Los Angeles Department of Military and Veteran Affairs.

Back cover photos courtesy of the author from the Los Angeles Maritime Museum.

Cover Graphics: Mike Egeler, Egeler Design
Typography: Janyce J. Taylor

PICTORIAL HISTORIES PUBLISHING CO., INC.
713 South Third Street West, Missoula, Montana 59801
Phone (406) 549-8488   FAX (406) 728-9280
phpc@montana.com

TABLE OF CONTENTS

ABOUT THE AUTHOR

Harvey M. Beigel, author of the *U.S.S. Los Angeles (CA 135): Cold War Sentinel,* retired in 1991 after having taught 35 years in the Los Angeles City Schools and Los Angeles City College. As a teacher at Venice High School, he served as Department Chairman of Social Studies and as a consultant for the College Board's Advanced Placement program. Mr. Beigel served in the United States Air Force during the Korean War. His first book *Battleship Country: The Battle Fleet at San Pedro–Long Beach California – 1919-1940,* was published in 1983. This was followed by *The Fleet's In: Hollywood Presents the U.S. Navy in World War II,* published in 1994. He has also written several articles on naval history in the U.S. Naval Institute's *Proceedings, Sea Classics* magazine *Warship International, the Journal of the American Aviation Historical Society* and *Alert,* the official publication of the Fort MacArthur Military Museum, located in San Pedro, California. He is a member of the Los Angeles Maritime Museum in San Pedro and the San Pedro Bay Historical Society. Mr. Beigel, a native of Los Angeles, resides with his wife Elizabeth in Rancho Palos Verdes, California.

Harvey M. Beigel

WHAT'S IN A NAME?
Ships Called *LOS ANGELES*

In the course of the twentieth century, there have been seven ships named after the city of Los Angeles, California, the nation's second largest city. The most widely known of these ships is the heavy cruiser *USS Los Angeles* (CA–135), the first naval surface–combatant designated by that name. Described as "The Pacific Fleet's Glamour Girl" by the local press, the cruiser had gained notoriety as the focus of a Los Angeles county–wide war bond drive during World War II. The drive raised over $80,000,000 for the construction of the ship, twice the desired goal. During her 18 years of praiseworthy service, a favorable press kept local citizens informed about the cruiser's activities.

The dirigible ZR–3 was also named the *USS Los Angeles* when the 658–foot airship was christened by then first lady Mrs. Grace Coolidge in 1924. Manufactured by the Zeppelin Company in Friedrichshafen, Germany, the airship was turned over to the U.S. Navy as part of war reparations owed the United States. The American people went "Zeppelin mad" when they read newspaper stories about the release of peace doves from inside the airship during the christening ceremony. Excitement reigned when they learned that the water in the christening bottles was imported from the Jordan River as a gesture to the burning social issue of the time—prohibition. (1)

While accommodations on the airship for twenty people were described as sumptuous, and the 81 and 1/2 hour flight from Germany to the United States mesmerized the public, Rear Admiral William F. Moffett and others began planning operational experiments for the dirigible. Moffett, the Navy's foremost proponent of lighter–than–air aircraft (LTA), strongly believed that the airship could become a scouting ship for the fleet, but he and other naval dirigible enthusiasts were disheartened by a series of airship disasters in the 1920s. The airship *USS Shenandoah* (ZRS–1) crashed in three pieces in a violent storm in Ohio in 1925. Fourteen crewmen were killed when the control car and after section of the hull fell directly to the ground. Even worse for the champions of the Navy's lighter–than–air program was the crash of the *USS Akron* (ZRS–4) on April 4, 1933. Among the 73 fatalities was the father of naval rigid–airships himself Admiral Moffett.

Airship USS Los Angeles *(ZR–3) as she rests on the mast of the* USS Patoka *(AO–9), 1931.* U.S. Navy

While the *Los Angeles* (ZR–3) had some misfortunes herself, they were only minor. On one occasion in 1926, the combined effect of wind and cold air gave buoyancy to the ship's stern which pulled the airship, with 25 men aboard, to a vertical position above the 158–foot mooring mast. Some witnesses felt the ship was going to twist the mast and plunge to earth, but a fortunate shift in the wind allowed the dirigible to return gently to her normal position with only slight damage. This event lead to the development of the smaller and more practical "stub" mast.

Though decommissioned in 1932, the *Los Angeles* proved to be the most successful naval airship of that era. In eight years of service, she completed 331 flights and accrued 4,398 hours in the air. In dozens of training hops aboard the *LA*, crewmen got valuable experience in ground handling and in–flight routines. Under Lieutenant Commander Charles. E. Rosendahl, the *Los Angeles*, in an effort to demonstrate that an aircraft carrier could be used successfully as an emergency fueling station, landed on the stern of the aircraft carrier *USS Saratoga* (CV–3) on a gusty wintry day without any special equipment.

Also developed on the *Los Angeles* were techniques and equipment to retrieve observation planes. The dirigible had a specially designed trapeze which hooked the planes to her underside. Lieutenant A.W. Gorton made the first successful hook–on landing aboard the *Los Angeles* on August 20, 1929. As a result, two subsequent rigid airships were designed as LTA air craft carriers. (2)

With the loss of the *Akron* in 1933, the *LA* was reactivated and used by the Navy for other experiments. In 1934 she was reconditioned and reinflated and acted as a full–scale test–bed and classroom but never flew again. Lasting longer than any of the other rigid dirigibles, the airship was scrapped in 1940, having had the "longest useful life of any rigid airship." (3)

Another important ship named in honor of the largest city in California was the nuclear attack submarine *USS Los Angeles* (SSN–688), commissioned on November 13, 1976. This submarine was the lead ship of the world's largest class of nuclear submarines, the *Los Angeles* class. There were 62 of these boats built, a number that was only surpassed by the older and less expensive Soviet *Whiskey*–class diesel boats. The large 360–foot submarine with a displacement of 6,080 tons was designed to counter the very fast Soviet *Victor*–class attack submarines. These *Los Angeles*–class boats were about five knots faster than the older American *Sturgeon*–class attack boats but were much more expensive. The last improved *LA*–class submarine authorized by the Navy was the *USS Cheyenne* (SSN–773), launched in 1994 at a cost of $732.9 million dollars. The improved submarines had 12 vertical–launch tubes fitted forward which could fire Harpoon and Tomahawk cruise missiles. The earlier *Los Angeles*–class boats were later upgraded with quieting machinery and mining and undersea ice operating capabilities. (4)

During the Reagan years plans were developed to have these submarines act together in large numbers to form a barrier designed to stop Soviet subs from leaving their northern bases if war in Europe broke out. It was understood that the mission of these Soviet attack submarines would be to try to destroy

Attack submarine USS Los Angeles *(SSN–688), lead boat of the largest class of nuclear submarines, in the Atlantic ocean, June 1976.* U.S. Navy

NATO's resupply efforts. These American attack submarines would lie in wait along a Greenland–Iceland–United Kingdom line and at certain checkpoints in the northern Pacific to stop Soviet attacks on Allied shipping. At the same time, their presence would make Soviet strategic missile submarines (SSBNs) vulnerable to American attack as they moved out to sea. (5)

The foremost proponent of the *Los Angeles*–class submarine was Admiral Hyman Rickover, "father of the nuclear navy." Other specialists wanted different designs and had disdain for the expensive *Los Angeles*–class submarine. Rickover looked for political support when opponents wanted to kill the entire program. He was able to win over powerful Congressman Chet Holifield of California and Senator John Stennis of Mississippi. In a compromise, Congress chose the *LA*–class attack submarine, not on the basis of speed alone but on other characteristics. After Congress authorized the building of the lead boat, Rickover rewarded Representative Holifield by naming it the *USS Los Angeles* (SSN–688). This played well in Holifield's Los Angeles district. (6)   After over twenty–five years of ser-

vice, the submarine *USS Los Angeles* (SSN–688) was scheduled for decommissioning in the late 1990s. This led to discussions about the possibility of bringing the submarine to the Los Angeles Maritime Museum in San Pedro, California, as a floating exhibit. Decommissioning was put off, however, when the Navy proposed extending the life of the submarine with a new and more powerful reactor. (7)

There were two passenger ships which sailed under the name of *City of Los Angeles*. Both of them had been known by three or more different names in the course of their use, and both came to tragic ends, thus reviving the old sailor's adage that, "It's bad luck to change the name of a ship." The first of these ships was the North German Lloyd liner *Grosser Kurfurst* which was seized in an American port when the United States entered World War I. Under the new name *Aeolus,* the former German liner transported American troops to Europe, making eight voyages in 1917. The liner also made seven crossings bringing back troops in 1919. (8) After the war, she was operated by the Los Angeles Steamship Company (LASSCO) and

USS Aeolus (NO. 3005) *The former German liner* Grosser Kurfurst *was seized by the American government during World War I. Seen here serving as an American troopship, 1918.* U.S. NAVY

USS Aeolus *became the* City of Los Angeles *after the war. Seen here in Los Angeles Harbor in 1924.*
LEON CALLOWAY COLLECTION

the Matson line. Outfitted with luxurious accommodations and a new name, the *City of Los Angeles* became a big attraction in the 1920s and 1930s, carrying more than 80,000 passengers on Pacific cruises. Outperformed by newer and more modern vessels, she was sold to a San Diego firm which turned her into a night club and hotel. No longer the *City of Los Angeles*, she was given the nondescript name plate "*Show Boat*" in 1935. Finally in 1937, the worn–out ship was loaded with discarded iron and steel and sent to Japan for scrapping. (9)

A 16,000–ton, steel–hulled, cargo ship once also named *City of Los Angeles* came to a more honorable end. Built in 1918 as the *Victorious* in Alameda, California, she was placed in the trans–Atlantic service after World War I. After being acquired by the Panama–Pacific Line, she sailed between New York City and Los Angeles. It was during this period that she picked up two new names, first the *City of Havre* and later the *City of Los Angeles*. Just before the United States entered World War II, she became a Navy transport ship and was renamed the *USS George F. Elliot* (AP–13) after a Spanish–American War hero. On August 7, 1942, she landed elements of the First Marine Division on Guadalcanal Island in the Solomons. On the next day, Japanese torpedo bombers attacked the landing site, and one of the bombers coming in low was hit several times by *George F. Elliot's* antiaircraft guns. Unfortunately, the bomber crashed and exploded on the transport amidships. With fires raging out of control, the gutted ship was sunk the same day by Allied forces. (10)

One of the most attractive ships to be named *Los Angeles* was a Swedish motor ship operated by the Johnson Line. Rakish and fast, she made her maiden voyage in 1948 to engage in the Pacific Coast–European trade. She was fitted with 14 electric cranes for quick on– and off–loading. The 450–foot vessel had accommodations for ten or twelve people described as "just short of luxurious." (11) Demand for the services of these kinds of ships, however, declined with the growing popularity of cruise ships and container ships in the 1960s.

The final vessel bearing the name *Los Angeles* was a 10,000–ton Union Oil Company tanker. Built in San Francisco in 1916, she was acquired by the Navy and made two cruises with the Atlantic Train force during World War I and four transatlantic runs out of east coast ports. Back on the Pacific coast after the war, she made regular calls at west coast and foreign ports for over 25 years. Old and unable to compete with the larger tankers coming on line, she was sold by Union Oil to a Mexican company. Her fate was scarcely known even by "old timers," and by the late 1950s it was not known whether she was even afloat. The last word heard at Union Oil's Harbor Terminal concerned her new name; it had been changed to *Toteco*. (12)

Thus of the seven ships mentioned above, three of them were built and served specifically as ships in the United States Navy as a heavy cruiser, a dirigible and a nuclear submarine; three were once civilian ships but served with the Navy in wartime. The last ship named *Los Angeles* was a Swedish motor ship which came to the West Coast after World War II.

The cruiser *USS Los Angeles* was the best known of all the ships and dear to the hearts of Angelenos, because she was paid for by war bonds purchased by local citizens and served the Navy well. Research and development aboard the dirigible *USS Los Angeles* (ZR–3) helped enlarge the Navy's understanding of LTA warfare, paving the way for U–boat killer blimps during World War II. The success of the nuclear attack submarine *USS Los Angeles* (SSN–168)–class helped win the Cold War, and many are still in service in the late 1990s. A former German liner, a California built cargo ship and an oil tanker served in America's wars and also had memorable civilian careers including periods when they were known by the name *City of Los Angeles* or *SS Los Angeles*. The Swedish motor ship *Los Angeles* is in a class by herself.

END NOTES

(1)   John Toland, *The Great Dirigibles: Their Triumphs and Disasters* (New York: Dover Publications, 1957), p. 225. William F. Althoff, *Sky Ships: A History of the Airship in the United States Navy* (New York: Orion Books, 1990), p. xii.

(2)   Toland, *ibid.* p. 227.; Althoff, *ibid.*, p. 80.

(3)   Althoff, *op. cit* p. xii.

(4)   Norman Polmar, *The Naval Institute Guide to the Ships and Aircraft of the U.S. Fleet* (Annapolis: Naval Institute Press, 1997), p. 69.

(5)   Robert J. Love, Jr., *History of the U.S. Navy, 1942–1991, Vol. Two* (Harrisburg: Stackpole Books, 1992), pp. 611–12.

(6)   *Ibid.* pp. 616–17.

(7)   Interview with Dr. William Lee, Director of the Los Angeles Maritime Museum, San Pedro, CA., March 17, 1999.

(8)   *Dictionary of American Naval Fighting Ships, Vol. One* (Washington: Naval History Division, 1964), pp. 14–15.

(9)   "Los Angeles' Name Given Many Ships, *Los Angeles Times*, June 2, 1957.

(10)   *Dictionary of American Naval Fighting Ships, Vol. Three* (Washington: Naval History Division, 1977), p. 76.

(11)   *Los Angeles Times, op. cit.*

(12)   *Ibid.*

Attack transport USS Elliot (AP–13) *was once called the* City of Los Angeles *before she entered the Navy in 1940. Seen here off Norfolk Navy Yard, January 1, 1942.*

BONDS AWAY

For most of the twentieth century cruisers were described as warships which had less armor and firepower than the heavier battleships. Smaller and faster, they were cheaper to build and operate. In 1958 one surface warfare specialist defined the ship type in the following way: "Cruisers are small sisters of battleships with roughly similar roles, primarily having to do with surface and antiaircraft gunnery." (1)

At the beginning of the Second World War, there were approximately 40 cruisers in the United States Navy, both light (CLs) and heavy (CAs). Cruisers were named after American cities, bringing a source of pride to the communities for which they were named. Los Angeles, California, then the fourth largest city in the United States, did not have a cruiser honoring its name. There was, however, the dirigible the *USS Los Angeles* (ZR–3), which was taken out of service in 1932, but remained in the naval inventory until 1939.

Treaty limitations and budgetary constraints had made the building and naming of new cruisers relatively infrequent. This changed with the advent of World War II when the construction of cruisers became a high priority. It was natural that civic leaders around the country wanted one of the new cruisers named after their city.

This desire was especially true in southern California, an area with a rich history of naval activity. For over two decades, Los Angeles Harbor (San Pedro) and Long Beach had been the primary anchorage of the battleships and cruisers of the United States Fleet. It was from these two ports in Los Angeles county that the United States Fleet sailed to Pearl Harbor, Hawaii, in 1940. These were the same ships that were attacked on December 7, 1941. (2)

The possibility of building a cruiser *USS Los Angeles* became a reality when the United States Treasury Department began personalizing the sale of war bonds by permitting local governments to sponsor special war bond campaigns. It was believed that people could more readily identify with a bond drive that was geared to the "purchase" of specific airplanes, naval vessels or other military equipment. It was correctly assumed that this kind of program would stimulate interest in

Model of the USS Los Angeles *at the MGM Motion Picture Studios in Culver City, California, on July 3, 1943.* LA PUBLIC LIBRARY

the war effort, bring the actuality of the war closer to the civilian population and allow families with sons, brothers and fathers in the service to help win the war. (3) The people of Los Angeles yearned to have a ship named after their city. In this instance, the Treasury Department did not need to depend primarily on war propaganda to promote the war bond sale. The Drive was mainly an appeal to civic pride which inspired citizens to take an active role in the bond campaign. In July 1943 a special bond drive to raise $40,000,000 for the construction of the heavy cruiser *USS Los Angeles* was begun in Los Angeles county with the slogan, "Buy an extra bond in July."

Wartime patriotism and civic pride were two of the key elements in the success of this month–long event. A local newspaper advertisement put it this way: "Today no fighting ship bears the name of this great county with its miles of coast line facing the battleground of the Pacific...." With the cruisers *Houston, San Francisco* and *Boise* having already been under fire, "Los Angeles too must have a ship proudly to carry its name in the winning fight for freedom." (4)

The kickoff of the bond drive occurred on July 1, 1943, with a massive rally at the Hollywood Bowl. Special bond sales booths were set up at the entrances. Over 20,000 people listened to Secretary of the Navy Frank Knox discuss America's latest successes in the Pacific. The next day, bond drive director Albert S. Scott announced, "We would like to see 1,000,000 Los Angeles County citizens acquire a personal interest in the cruiser." Favorable sales were reported that very day. The War Savings staff immediately began canvassing 92 Los Angeles county communities. In a news account on July 3, the fervor over the drive to build the cruiser reached such a level as to spur the unlikely report that the crew of the new warship would probably be "from the city which it is named." A bit less exaggerated was the notion that the bond drive was to be coordinated with a recruiting program to enlist 1,000 women into the WAVES It was reported that these recruits would replace men at shore stations for duty on the new cruiser *Los Angeles*. (5)

A window display in a downtown Los Angeles store featuring an original drawing of the USS Los Angeles *by artist Arthur Beaumont, July 1943.* LA PUBLIC LIBRARY

Actress Joan Leslie christens a model of the USS Los Angeles *at the downtown Los Angeles May Company store on July 9, 1943.* LA PUBLIC LIBRARY

Respectfully dedicated to the U.S. Navy and the Los Angeles City Council

THE U.S.S. LOS ANGELES

Words and Music by
HAYDEN SIMPSON
and BUD AVERILL

"I am the hope of Los Angeles"

"I am a throbbing ship of steel and drive, straining to do my part in the battle for peace. I can be a lightning power to destroy the enemy! I *may* be a decisive factor in a sea battle they may turn the tide toward a speedier Victory!"

"My power to help win this war depends on You—Mr. and Mrs. Los Angeles! Upon your vision in buying war bonds to build me, *now!* One extra bond purchased

by you *this* month—will buy my driving, fighting force in the coming sea battles."

Make this your red letter day—go out and buy that extra War Bond today. Be proud for the rest of your life that you were instrumental in building the good ship—U.S.S. Cruiser Los Angeles!

The Lyon Van & Storage Company gladly donates this space to remind you of the great part Los Angeles can play, in the invitation of Uncle Sam.

Lyon Van and Storage advertisement "I am the hope of Los Angeles." *LA TIMES* JULY 27, 1943

BUY WAR BONDS

Build the Battle Cruiser

"U.S.S. LOS ANGELES"

"above and beyond the call of duty"

MIGHT
TO MATCH
OUR MEN!

We've sent thousands of our men into the Navy. Now we can show these men that we are behind them 100%—that by buying extra War Bonds we will be doing our best to match their fortitude and courage, under fire. Let's prove we are fighting with them by putting the U.S.S. Los Angeles and other sister ships on the high seas!

NEGRO WAR SAVINGS COMMITTEE

2512 South Central Avenue

The Black community of Los Angeles joins the bond drive. *LA Times,* JULY 27, 1943

IT'S IN YOUR HANDS

"It's in your hand. Insure the future, buy war bonds." *LA Times,* July 29, 1943.

HELP BUILD The Cruiser LOS ANGELES-
BUY an *EXTRA* WAR BOND in JULY !

Typical advertisement. *LA TIMES* JULY 1, 1943

THE MORE WAR BONDS YOU BUY...THE QUICKER THEY DIE

BUY AN EXTRA WAR BOND IN JULY TO
BUILD THE CRUISER "LOS ANGELES"

C.H.Baker
QUALITY FOOTWEAR SINCE 1899

C.H. Baker Shoe Store advertisement "The more bonds you buy...the quicker they die." *LA TIMES* JULY 8, 1943

Words and music
to the song
The USS Los Angeles.
SAN PEDRO HISTORICAL
SOCIETY

N. Highland Ave., Hollywood
Printed in U.S.A.
public performance for profit.

8

Enthusiasm for the bond drive gathered momentum with many different elements of the city and county. Local chambers of commerce, industrial establishments, unions, merchants, and city and county government agencies vigorously supported and contributed to the drive. The city's major newspapers, the *Los Angeles Times* and the *Los Angeles Examiner,* along with many other local newspapers, covered the drive daily. Foremost among those working actively in the drive was a group of downtown Los Angeles businessmen. Calling themselves "Retailers for Victory," this group was instrumental in setting up a Victory House in Pershing Square in downtown Los Angeles as the rallying point for the bond drive. Banners and buntings were also placed along major downtown streets. Many stores sold bonds on their premises.

Advertisers took out ads on a daily basis informing the public about the *USS Los Angeles* bond drive. For example, an ad for the C.H. Baker shoe stores showed Hitler, Mussolini and a cobra-like Japanese image hanging by rope over a picture of the cruiser with the admonition, "The More War Bonds You Buy...The Quicker They Die." In a full-page ad on July 16, the May Company department store asked customers to buy an extra war bond to finance the cruiser *Los Angeles* so that, "We Will Be in on the Kill" in destroying the Axis Powers. In another advertisement by a local van and storage company, the *Los Angeles Times* displayed a picture of the yet to be built cruiser *Los Angeles* with the inscription, "I Am the Hope of Los Angeles." (6)

The bond drive brought Angelenos of diverse backgrounds together in this common cause. The Native Daughters of the Golden West sold war bonds at the large Barker Bros. Furniture Store in downtown Los Angeles. The Junior Auxiliary of the Jewish Home for the Aged offered bonds specifically to purchase the ship's galley, bake shop, doctor and dentist offices. The Negro War Savings Committee informed readers that after sending "thousands of our men into the Navy," Negroes wanted to back their men by buying an extra war bond to put "the *USS Los Angeles* and other sister ships on the high seas." (7) Fishermen and watermen, notably with Yugoslavian, Ital-ian, Mexican, Scandinavian and Greek backgrounds, purchased large numbers of war bonds in San Pedro. The goal for the entire maritime industry, including fishermen, shipbuilders and unions was set at $1,000,000. (8) While Japanese–American groups in Hawaii participated in war bond drives, the evacuation of the Japanese–Americans from the Los Angeles area to relocation camps precluded any such activity by them.

The city's movie industry brought an added dimension to the bond drive not available in other communities. The marketing skills of the movie studios and the stars themselves brought glamour and color to the war bond drive for the cruiser *Los Angeles*. Metro–Goldwyn Mayer (MGM) studios donated a twenty–five foot scale model of the heavy cruiser, and screen actress Dale Evans christened the model on July 4, 1943, in Pershing Square. Beautifully crafted by studio model–makers, Treasury officials planned to tow the replica to as many as eighty–four communities in the county as was possible. Not to be outdone, a twenty–six foot replica of the ship was donated by Republic Studios to promote the sale of bonds and to recruit WAVES. An even larger (35–foot) replica of the ship was launched in a ceremony at the May Company department store in downtown Los Angeles. Actress Joan Leslie smashed a bottle of champagne on the ship's prow as Deputy Mayor of Los Angeles Orville Caldwell announced to onlookers, "We will put Los Angeles city limit signs" on the "four corners of the earth" when the real cruiser is launched. Also on hand for the festivities were actresses Eleanor Parker and Faye Emerson. (9) While Oscar Levant and Clifton Fadiman tossed out quiz questions at a Pershing Square rally, Mary Pickford, Ava Gardener and Vickie Lane sparked a rally at the exclusive I. Magnin women's store. Over $350,000 worth of bonds were sold there in one day. Purchasers received autographed lithographs of the cruiser *Los Angeles* by artist Arthur Beaumont.

By July 14, the bond drive reached $18,675,000 in purchases at the drive's halfway point, with reports that $1,500,000 a day was forthcoming county–wide. To further stimulate sales, bond drive strategists proclaimed each Thursday as the day to buy specific parts of the ship with their bond purchases. For

example, $100,000 collected on July 11 went for the laying of the ship's keel (the actual keel was laid on July 28 at the Philadelphia Navy Yard). Other special items underwritten by bond sales were boilers, turbines, triple 8–inch gun turrets and sick bay equipment. To further spur the drive, the *Los Angeles Times* on July 18 listed a number of other items for the ship that were still lacking. The goals for sponsorship of various items in terms of dollar prices proved to be somewhat of a headache in these campaigns nationwide because actual costs varied around the country. By agreement with the armed forces, the War Finance Division of the Treasury Department had to settle on average or symbolic costs of the items. (10) To keep the momentum of the drive going, a *Times* editorial warned readers not to fall under the spell of lethargy and inattention. Appealing to civic pride once again, a Desmonds Men's Store advertisement pleaded with citizens to furnish the money to "send our name into battle shoulder–to–shoulder with San Francisco and other cities so honored" and added, "From a lack of a few dollars we might actually be shamed for years to come." (11) In an editorial that very next day, the *Times* told its readers prophetically that even if the war were over tomorrow, "We would still want the cruiser *Los Angeles*." (12) The fact is that

the cruiser *USS Los Angeles* (CA–135) was not ready for sustained action until World War II was almost over. She did, however, serve with distinction during the Cold War from 1946 to 1963.

By July 31, 1943, all kinds of sales ideas were put into play to attain the $40,000,000. One of the final efforts to stimulate interest in attaining the drive's goal was the auctioning off of a small jail from Harvard, Nebraska, donated by a teenage boy. The bidding was held at Pershing Square where ventriloquist Edgar Bergen and his "dummy" Charlie McCarthy of radio fame, bought the "pokey" for "$10,000 and seventy–five cents." It was reported by day's end that purchases from all over Los Angeles county had been oversubscribed above the drive's goal of $40 million. The 31–day drive for the cruiser had in fact raised $80,371,372. This was enough to finance the construction of the heavy cruiser *USS Los Angeles* and four destroyers. In a gesture to the city of Los Angeles, the Navy said it would name the destroyers after local heroes who had died in combat. (13)

Further cementing the city to the fortunes of the new heavy cruiser was the launching of the ship by the wife of the Mayor of Los Angeles, Mrs. Fletcher Bowron, on August 20, 1944. Surmounted on a decorated stand was a big black and gold shield

Mayor of Los Angeles and his wife, the christener, July 27, 1945. H.R. CARVER

Commissioning picture of the crew, July 27, 1945. H.R. CARVER

inscribed with the words, "This fighting ship sponsored and made possible by the bond purchases of the people of Los Angeles." In his final words, the Mayor of Los Angeles Fletcher Bowron presented the ship's Welfare fund $7,000 contributed by city employees and school children and announced that athletic equipment for the ship's gymnasium would be given by the California Athletic Commission. (14) Commenting on the christening, Los Angeles columnist Bill Henry wrote:

Our cruiser, the USS Los Angeles *was christened .....today and in keeping with the best California tradition, the occasion was awash with superlatives from the opening toot of the bugle until Mrs. Bowron capped the climax with a mighty clout that sprayed California champagne over the vicinity.* (15)

The large number of "Angelenos" in attendance, including California's two United States Senators, were thrilled to see the 13,000-ton warship float for the first time in the huge drydock at the Philadelphia Navy Yard.

The *USS Los Angeles* (CA–135) was commissioned on July 22, 1945. Her capabilities were first tested in the Caribbean Sea during September and October 1945 where she completed her "shakedown cruise" off Guantanamo Bay, Cuba. Between October 1 and 15, the new cruiser went through extensive gunnery and ship handling drills. After being accepted by the Navy, the heavy cruiser proceeded to Terminal Island (Los Angeles Harbor), California, for a post shakedown overhaul.

PLANK OWNERS' CERTIFICATE

U. S. S. LOS ANGELES

HARRY ROSCOE CARVER Jr.

WAS A MEMBER OF THE ORIGINAL CREW WHICH COMMISSIONED THIS VESSEL AND IS THEREFORE ENTITLED TO ALL THE RIGHTS AND PRIVILEGES OF A PLANK OWNER ON SAID SHIP INCLUDING A CLEAR AND UNENCUMBERED TITLE TO ONE PLANK IN THE WEATHER DECK.

DATE OF COMMISSIONING
22 July 1945

CAPTAIN, U. S. NAVY, COMMANDING

A Plank Owner's certificate issued on the day of commissioning. H.R. CARVER

Large Crowd Attends Commissioning of USS Los Angeles

"Top left shows the officers and crew of the 13,000-ton cruiser USS LOS ANGELES during the commissioning ceremonies here last Sunday."

12

END NOTES

(1)   Roy S. Benson, "Fleet Air Defense: Vital New Role of the Cruiser," *United States Naval Institute Proceedings*, June 1958, p. 47.

(2)   Harvey M. Beigel, "The Battlefleet's Home Port: 1919–1940," *United States Naval Institute Proceedings, Historical Supplement*, 1985, pp. 54-63.

(3)   John Morton Blum, *V Was for Victory: Politics and Culture During World War II* (New York: Harcourt Brace Jovanovich, 1976), p. 20.

(4)   *San Pedro News–Pilot*, July 3, 1943.

(5)   *Los Angeles Times,* July 3, 1943.

(6)   *Ibid.*, July 27, 1943.

(7)   *Ibid.*, July 22, 1943.

(8)   *San Pedro News–Pilot,* July 1, 1943.

(9)   *Los Angeles Times,* July 9, 1943

(10)   Jarvis M. Morse, *Paying for a World War: The United States Financing World War II* (Washington: Government Printing Office, 1971), p. 215.

(11)   *Los Angeles Times,* July 26, 1943.

(12)   *Ibid.*, July 27, 1943.

(13)   *San Pedro News–Pilot*, July 13, 1951.

(14)   *Los Angeles Examiner*, August 20, 1944.

(15)   *Los Angeles Times,* June 3, 1957.

Philadelphia, Pa., Friday, July 27, 1945

"Top right is a section of the large crowd which attended."

"*Wherever the* USS LOS ANGELES *puts into port, a new city limits will be established*," *is pointed out here by Machinist William E. Hicks and Lt. Comdr. James H. Elson, both Los Angeles residents. On the top gun turret, E.J. Martinez helped chalk the sign as the ship anchored in Guantanamo Bay, Cuba, on its shakedown cruise, September 10, 1945.* U.S. NAVY

FROM THE CHINA STATION TO DEACTIVATION

The *USS Los Angeles* arrived in Shanghai, China, for service with the 7th Fleet on January 3, 1946. In those early post-war days, the fleet's operating area included South China, East China and the Yellow Sea. Rear Admiral C. Turner Joy, formerly the commander of the Yangtze Patrol force, took over as the commander of Task Force 74 aboard his flagship the *USS Los Angeles* on January 15. Among his tasks were to maintain control of the navigable portions of the Yangtze river and to establish and operate mobile base facilities afloat and port facilities ashore on the China coast. While Tsingtao in the north became the primary fleet anchorage in China, Shanghai and Hong Kong became secondary support bases in the south. At that time, some 7,000 Army and 6,000 Navy personnel began arriving in Shanghai in support of American efforts to sea–lift anti–communist forces (nationalist) to the north and facilitate the repatriation of remaining Japanese troops in the area. U.S. Navy landing craft shipped food up the Yangtze River to famine stricken Hunan Province and returned with cargoes of weapons and supplies for Chiang Kai–Schek's armies in Manchuria. Similar efforts were being undertaken in Hong Kong. The Navy also began training elements of Chiang's Navy at Tsingtao on the Shantung peninsula. (1)

The *Los Angeles* became the station ship on the Wangpoo River astride Shanghai's famous Bund. The cruiser patrolled the coast of south China but anchored regularly in Shanghai and Hong Kong. One naval historian wrote that in Shanghai "death and decay were everywhere" in that notorious town. Though the cruiser's medical staff never tired of treating exotic strains of venereal disease, they never got used to seeing river tug boats towing two or three Chinese bodies down river.

At times tug boats would tie the bodies to a buoy next to the cruiser where they lay until the end of the day when another tug towed them away. (2) Nor were American sailors immune from physical attack in the city. Knifings occurred in the so-called Blood Alley, and in one political demonstration on January 31, 1946, three sailors were severely beaten. (3)

Shortly after RADM Joy came aboard, the *Los Angeles* sailed for the British Crown Colony of Hong Kong where considerable

The USS Los Angeles *arrives in Hong Kong from Shanghai on February 7, 1946.* LOS ANGELES EXAMINER (USC SPEC. COLL)

sea–lift activity of nationalist forces was underway. Once the pearl of the Orient, Hong Kong was then a devastated city recovering from over four years of war. The crew of the *LA* had access to what was once one of the great liberty ports in the world. Unfortunately on March 28, 1946, the cruiser was quarantined in the harbor after two cases of smallpox were diagnosed on board. (4) Sea;oft activities in Kowloon were completed by the end of May. Under the auspices of the 7th Fleet, it was estimated that 251,976 of Chiang Kai–Schek's troops and 5,220 horses ferried out.

In 1946 China was entering into the final stage of the civil war between the nationalists (KMT) under Chiang Kai Shek and the communists (CCP) led by Mao Tse Tung. With greater focus on the defense of Europe and little confidence in Chiang Kai Shek's corrupt regime in some quarters, the United States was unsteady in its support of the KMT. American policy makers followed a contradictory policy of trying to end the civil war by brokering a nationalist–communist coalition while at the same time reestablishing Chiang's authority in northern China at the expense of the CCP. In the north over 50,000 U.S. marines were busy disarming and repatriating Japanese troops while guarding strategically valuable coal mines. For a time those endeavors turned out to be less problematic than containing the internecine fighting between the KMT and the CCP. General George C. Marshall arrived in China to arrange a peaceful settlement between Chiang and the communists, but relations with the Chinese communists deteriorated when they accused the United States Navy of aiding the nationalist military effort against them. Despite complaints, 7th Fleet transports continued to carry KMT forces to the north. Marshall found it impossible to work out an accommodation between the two sides. When the communists began attacking marines near the principal American naval base in Tsingtao, killing eight leathernecks in an ambush nearby, the American position became tenuous. With the threat of mass communist junk attacks looming just twelve miles north of the base and the communists firing on U.S. flying boats in the bay, the *Los Angeles* and five destroyers were dispatched to Tsingtao harbor on June

15. (5) Because delicate negotiations were then underway between the parties, no shots were fired at the CCP bands by this formidable naval force. The *Los Angeles* trained her 8–inch guns menacingly on the surrounding hills. The cruiser did fire her 20–mm guns at some floating mines in the area presumably left by the Japanese. (6) It is not known to what degree the presence of the *Los Angeles* and her escorts had on persuading the communists to halt their attacks, but a temporary cease fire was entered upon between the KMT and the CCP forces.

In late 1946 American naval forces were strengthened at Tsingtao, bringing the force up to 38 combat ships. (7) Tsingtao was an isolated outpost, however, and finally fell to the victorious communists in 1949 when CCP troops captured the countryside surrounding the base. The U.S. Navy had already left by that time. With continuing mass defections to the communists by Chiang's army in the north, one American naval officer commented, "We'd take them up to Chinwangtao, and the Chinese communists were very close, and they (the transported

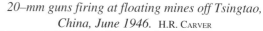

20–mm guns firing at floating mines off Tsingtao, China, June 1946. H.R. CARVER

Curtiss SC–1 Seahawk *ready to take off from port catapult, June 1946.* H.R. CARVER

USS Los Angeles making a landing area for returning floatplane. H.R. CARVER

Curtiss SC–1 *airborne, June 1946.* H.R. CARVER

Damaged Seahawk *on* Los Angeles *on the Wang Po river, Shanghai, China. An upstream freighter had lost her anchor and came to rest alongside the cruiser.* H.R. CARVER

Nationalists) would go over and surrender.... It was discouraging." (8) President Harry Truman had had enough. In February 1949 all remaining American soldiers and sailors were withdrawn from China.

The *Los Angeles* remained in Chinese waters for most of 1946. It was not an easy deployment. While at anchor on the Wang Po river, a freighter upstream lost her anchor and killed several Chinese in Bum boats. The freighter then came to rest alongside the *Los Angeles*, damaging a Curtiss SC–1 Seahawk floatplane on a stern catapult. (9) After another accident which damaged the ship's stern–tube bearing, the cruiser had to limp all the way back to Pearl Harbor for repairs. There were no nearby repair facilities available in the area. A second stern tube bearing gave out only three weeks after the *LA* returned to Shanghai as flagship of Cruiser Division 3. Rather than wait for the arrival of the permanent flagship, the *USS Columbus* (CA–74), the pride of the "City of the Angels" was ordered to cut short her Asian tour and return to the United States. Naval leaders had decided to advance her routine overhaul period in order to take care of her emergency repairs. The *Los Angeles* arrived at Hunters Point Naval Shipyard in San Francisco on January 20, 1947, three months in advance of her normal overhaul period. (10) After a three–month overhaul, the *Los Angeles* returned to Los Angeles Harbor where she was met by local dignitaries including the mayor of Los Angeles and the Sheriff of Los Angeles County, both influential figures in the 1943 bond drive. Soon after, the heavy cruiser was ordered back to San Francisco and the Pacific Reserve Fleet. The "darling" of Los Angeles, in the company of countless other fighting ships, was ordered "mothballed" by the cost–conscious Navy.

One local newspaper contrasted the *Los Angeles*' departure for the Bay area and deactivation with a more stirring period in the cruiser's history, "There were no speeches, such as graced the launching of the mighty $40,000,000 warship. No bands played martial music, nor even a dirge." The life of the ship seemed over. Accompanying the *Los Angeles* was her sister ship, the heavy cruiser *USS Bremerton* (CA–130), also destined for deactivation. The Navy announced that it no longer had the personnel to man these 13,000–ton ships. Perhaps to allay any anger about the *LA's* fate, the Navy told one local newspaper that the cruiser would merely be smeared in grease which "could be blasted from her armament and made ready to fight in a few hours." Decommissioned on April 9, 1948, the *LA* remained in its protective cocoons for two and a half years until called back for duty in the Korean War in late 1950. (11)

USS Los Angeles *undergoing the first phase of reactivation at the San Francisco Naval Shipyard, December 5, 1950.* Los Angeles Examiner (USC Spec. Coll.)

17

END NOTES

(1)   United States Pacific Fleet, Commander United States Naval Forces, Western Pacific, *Narrative of Seventh Fleet*, 1 September 1945 to 1 October 1946, p. 8. Samuel J. Cox, USN, *U.S. Naval Strategy and Foreign Policy in China, 1945–1950* (Annapolis: A Trident Scholar Project Report, 1980), p. 56.

(2)   Michael T. Eisenberg, *Shield of the Republic: The United States Navy in an Era of Cold War and Violent Peace, 1945–1962, Vol. I* (New York: St. Martin's Press, 1993), p. 128.

(3)   *New York Times,* January 5, 1946.

(3)   *Ibid.*, March 28, 1946.

(4)   *Los Angeles Examiner,* March 28, 1946.

(5)   *New York Times,* June 15, 1946.

(6)   Letter from *LA* crewman H.R. Carver, March 24, 1999.

(7)   *Los Angeles Times,* December 13, 1946.

(8)   Quoted in Stephen Howarth's *To Shining Sea: A History of the United States Navy, 1775–1991* (New York: Random House, 1991), p. 482.

(9)   Carver, *op. cit.*

(10)   *Los Angeles Times,* January 4, 1947.

(11)   *Los Angeles Examiner,* December 5, 1950.

Starboard engine room throttle station,
USS Los Angeles. H.R. Carver

USS LOS ANGELES (CA–135)
ON STATION IN KOREA

Budgetary and strategic considerations brought the drastic demobilization of America's sea forces at the end of World War II in 1945. On the eve of the Korean War in June 1950, the fleet had declined from almost 1,200 major combatants in 1945 to a mere 237. Personnel levels had shrunk from 3.4 million officers and men in the summer of 1945 to just one-tenth of the wartime peak.

Two major factors account for the United States' ability to expand its naval forces rapidly by two–thirds after the first year of the Korean War to a total of 1,100 ships. First, a number of relatively new warships from World War II lay "mothballed" in ports around the country. In the case of the *Los Angeles*, the reactivation process took less than two months. The *LA* was recommissioned January 27, 1951. (1) Secondly, the manning of these ships was accomplished by calling up 190,000 reservists, many of them veterans of World War II. Also available was a pool of 10,000 officer candidates in NROTC units in the nation's universities. The draft and the threat of induction into the army provided an ample number of seaman recruits. (2)

On December 5, 1950, the Navy announced the reactivation of the *USS Los Angeles* along with four other *Baltimore*-class heavy cruisers in the reserve fleet. Thus seven months after the communists invaded South Korea, the *Los Angeles* was recommissioned. Attending the ceremony on the cruiser's fantail were Fleet Admiral Chester A. Nimitz and Fletcher Bowron, Mayor of the city of Los Angeles. After a "shakedown" cruise, off San Diego, the heavy cruiser began training exercises off the California coast.

The *Baltimore*–class cruisers, of which there were fourteen, had one fewer triple–gun turret than the *Cleveland*–class (CL–55) light cruisers. Unlike the *Clevelands*, the completion during World War II of the *Baltimores* had not been rushed. Strong and stable hulls and a much longer design period in their construction made these cruisers less top–heavy than the light cruisers. Nine 8–inch (3x3) and twelve 5–inch (6x2) guns plus the twenty 3–inch antiaircraft guns added later made these *Baltimore*–class cruisers potent adversaries during the early years of the Cold War. The postwar era had given cruisers added importance as the upkeep of battleships proved so expensive. A *Baltimore*–class cruiser required a crew of only 1,100 men, an *Iowa*–class battleship 2,700. With the decline of battleship force numbers, cruisers handled many of the "heavy" shore bombardment tasks. (3)

In the age of nuclear weapons, carrier task forces were dispersed more widely. Cruisers were assigned the job screening against enemy surface raiders and carrying out long range scouting activities in bad weather. By 1948 the typical, fast carrier group of three carriers led a force consisting of six cruisers and sixteen destroyers. With ample space and communications equipment, cruisers frequently served as fleet flagships of these groups. The *Los Angeles* (CA–135) and two of her sister ships the *USS St. Paul* (CA–73) and the *USS Helena* (CA–75) had been converted into fleet flag ships, and their sister ships (CA–69,70,74 and 136) were later converted into guided missile ships. Of the units "mothballed" after the war, five *Baltimore*–class cruisers were recommissioned during the Korean Conflict, in

Citizens view the return of the cruiser Los Angeles *from the Reserve Fleet to Los Angeles Harbor, April 14, 1951.*
SAN PEDRO HISTORICAL SOCIETY

cluding the *Los Angeles*. (4) These heavy cruisers had a displacement of 13,600 tons standard weight and 17,200 tons when fully loaded. They were 664 feet long and were powered by four shaft–geared turbines allowing a top speed of 33 knots.

Before arriving on the east coast of Korea as the flagship of Cruiser Division Five on May 31, 1951, the *USS Los Angeles* spent her last day stateside at Wilmington (Los Angeles Harbor), California, on April 14, 1951. The connection between the ship and the city was reaffirmed there when the heavy cruiser was greeted by the wife of the mayor of Los Angeles Mrs. Fletcher Bowron, the ship's original christener. Also on hand were several civic leaders who had participated in the wartime bond drive almost seven years earlier plus an enthusiastic group of onlookers. Placed on the quarterdeck was a sign which would become a familiar symbol on the ship. It read, "Los Angeles City Limit, Population 1,971,841, Elevation 320 Feet." (5) The warship sailed for Korea that day. It is interesting to note that when Mayor Bowron and a group of California mayors later

Los Angeles Harbor looking east to Long Beach as it appeared in the 1950s. LA HARBOR DEPARTMENT

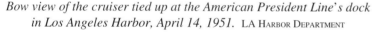

Bow view of the cruiser tied up at the American President Line's dock in Los Angeles Harbor, April 14, 1951. LA HARBOR DEPARTMENT

Stern view showing two twin gun mounts. LA HARBOR DEPARTMENT

visited the ship in Korea, Bowron spent the night on the *Los Angeles* in the war zone and was met with signs festooned all over the ship reading Los Angeles City limits.

Since the beginning of the Korean War, United Nations' naval forces led by the United States and Great Britain maintained control of the sea around the Korean peninsula with a blockade and interdiction campaign. The combined UN forces included all types of naval craft from ten different countries. Though the commitment of heavy ships to the fray was much less than it had been in World War II, all four *Iowa*–class fast battleships and several American 8–inch cruisers, including the *USS Los Angeles,* participated. When peace negotiations started in the summer of 1951 stabilized the fighting fronts, the United Nations' naval blockade and interdiction and air campaign remained the only UN offensive force operating in Korea. The goal of the UN naval and air forces was to continue to deny the communists the ability to resupply their forces along

Mayor Fletcher Bowron of Los Angeles and Captain Robert MacFarlane, CO of the cruiser Los Angeles, with the ubiquitous "city limit" sign in the background, April 1951.

This profile view of the cruiser tied up at the American President Line's dock in Los Angeles Harbor, April 14, 1951, shows the main 8–inch turrets.

Ceremony on the cruiser's quarterdeck in Los Angeles Harbor, April 1951. Los Angeles Examiner (USC SPECIAL COLLECION)

the battle front, then roughly at the 38th parallel. This line extended from Munsan in the west to Kosong in the east, but the combined UN naval and air strategy was careful not to pass the 39° 37" North parallel in the west or the 42° 05" parallel in the east. (6) Thus the blockade of the North Korean coastline was to stay clear of Soviet and Chinese territory. While the two communist powers denounced the continuing blockade, both observed it. The communists used mines, coastal shore batteries, limited air power and antiaircraft guns to protect the flow of military equipment south. While the Soviets had naval surface forces and approximately 80 submarines based in nearby Vladivostok, direct naval or air attacks on UN naval forces afloat never took place. Despite evidence that the extensive mining operations along the North Korean coasts were supervised by the Soviets and that anti–ship shore batteries were of Russian make, Russian submarines and aircraft were careful not to make aggressive moves against the UN forces. The UN blockade and interdiction effort prevented the communists from moving supplies by sea while siege and bombardment operations disrupted the communist land transportation system along the coasts.

The blockade was described by one authority on Korean War naval operations as a "crazy and mixed up" endeavor in which communist trucks and trains were chased by ships at sea. (7) There even was a "trainbuster" club in which ships whose gunfire had destroyed a train received certificates of commendation. Communist soldiers just 20 miles from the coast could feel the shock of naval guns while troops closer to the shore were maimed and demoralized by the constant shelling of their bunkers. With the important exception of one notable sortie to the west coast of Korea, the *USS Los Angeles* was assigned bombardment and interdiction duties on the east coast of Korea during her two deployments.

On the Korean east coast, the beaches were barren with coastal mountains rising from the sea. The currents and depths made the offshore coast suitable for drifter mines. For over 36 months of the war, UN ships on the east coast faced hidden shore defenses in tunneled, rocky hills. Many of the guns, usually in caves, were simple artillery pieces, 75–mm or 105–mm. Mines were always a threat. This bitter, unglamorous and seemingly futile sea war seemed to be the fate of UN surface task elements supporting UN troops on their front line flanks and laying siege to the city of Wonsan. The continuous daily bombardment and patrols, aimed both at disrupting enemy supply efforts and supporting UN infantry units, did not get the press attention that the carrier jet fighters did, but their activities helped prevent communist supplies from being moved by sea. It was only the massive efforts of the North

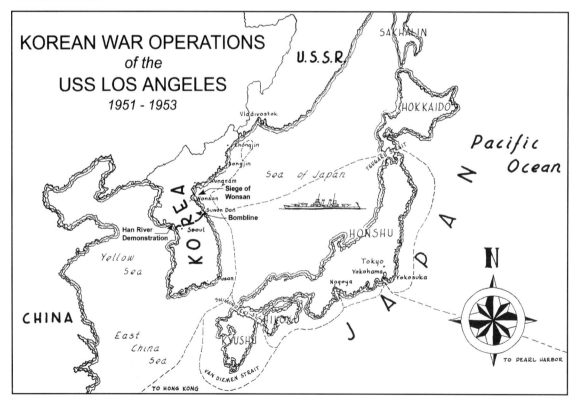

KOREAN WAR OPERATIONS
of the
USS LOS ANGELES
1951 - 1953

A view of the cruiser Los Angeles *from the air, March 21, 1951.* U.S. NAVY

Korean repair crews that kept the supply trucks and trains moving war material south.

A key area along the east coast, Wonsan received the utmost attention of the UN naval forces. This harbor city of 100,000 people was located about fifty miles north of the stalemated battle line. The city's strategic importance rested on the fact that it controlled all land traffic through the mouth of the Seoul–Wonsan corridor. Furthermore, one of the two north–south railroad lines and several east coast road systems ran through the city because narrow coastal plains and corrugated mountain ridges made that the only passageway to the front. This port city underwent the longest naval siege in history, lasting 861 days. (8) The mission of the UN naval forces to wear down this hub of the North Korean transportation network was not an easy task. Well–concealed communist guns and floating mines took their toll on the blockading ships.

Rear Admiral Arleigh A. Burke, the legendary destroyer hero of the Pacific War and future Chief of Naval Operations (CNO), came aboard the *USS Los Angeles* as Commander Cruiser Division Five (ComCruDiv5) at Pearl Harbor as the heavy cruiser headed for Korea in May 1951. It had already been demonstrated that heavy shelling was providing good cover for the UN's Eighth Army which had moved to better, more sustainable positions above the 38th parallel. Teaming up with two destroyer escorts, the *Los Angeles* became, for a time, the artillery support for the first Republic of Korea (ROK) Corps on the east coast. Impressed with the U.S. Navy's efficiency, ROK Vice Admiral Lee Song Ho later remarked, "Burke's gunfire support was so deliberate and effective that

friendly forces could easily resist enemy attacks along the coastline." (9) In contrast Burke was not entirely satisfied with the South Korean performance, believing that his naval "guns were too often aimed at poor targets." Moreover he believed that the ROK ground forces tended to be wasteful in their ordinance requests. Burke also wanted to establish the training of ground control parties for spotting and directing targeting.

For this reason, Burke visited 1st ROK Corps commander General Paik Sun Yup to see for himself what was happening at the front. Both came under enemy fire when Burke's alarm wristwatch went off unexpectedly. While no one was hit, Paik swore he would never take Burke out again. Later, at the end of a briefing shared with Lieutenant General James Van Fleet, Commander of the Eighth Army, Paik proudly but unexpectedly announced, "We will [now] hear a briefing from our artillery commander, Arleigh Burke." Without prior notice, Rear Admiral Burke very ably winged his way through an artillery briefing of sorts. (10)

The USS Los Angeles *pulls alongside the* USS New Jersey *(BB–62) off the coast of Korea to transfer RADM Arleigh A. Burke to the* New Jersey *for a conference, June 7, 1951.* U.S. Navy

Though Burke served as Cruiser Division Commander on the *LA* for only a month, his leadership had a lasting impression on those around him. For example, Burke suggested to Captain Robert MacFarlane, *Los Angeles'* Commanding Officer, a way of hitting an enemy bridge while also saving ordinance. He told the Captain it could be done by first aiming at both sides of the bridge's abutments. He demonstrated this when he bet MacFarlane he would buy him nine cases of scotch if he could hit a particular bridge with his first shot, eight with his second and so on. Burke's wager also stipulated, however, that for each missed shot over ten, MacFarlane was obliged to pay the admiral a bottle of scotch. After failing to make even one hit in thirty shots, MacFarlane got the point. Burke respectfully and kindly told MacFarlane, "It's hard to hit a bridge." The Commanding Officer of the *LA* then proceeded to make out an IOU for the twenty bottles of whiskey he owed Admiral Burke. (11)

Burke was able to get a helicopter and a pilot for use aboard the *Los Angeles* because of his good connections with the headquarters of the Commander–Naval forces, Far East (Com–NavFE). "Choppers" were proving to be extremely useful in Korea. They served as platforms for observation and gunfire spotting and for locating underwater mines. They also excelled in intership and shore transport, and Sea and Air rescue (SAR). Burke frequently flew to the front with MacFarlane or General Paik looking for targets. He also ordered some of his staff to visit ROK headquarters, ordering them to "take portable radios" with them to find out what the ROK needed at any given time and where his guns should direct their fire. (12)

On one occasion, Burke invited Lt. General Van Fleet to visit the *Los Angeles* for some ice cream after they had finished a battlefield conference. But the fifteen–minute flight to the ship almost ended in disaster when the young pilot came in too low and flipped the "chopper" over on the fantail of the cruiser. Fearing an explosion, sailors rushed to steady the battered helicopter until the passengers were out, then let it drop over the side. While battle–hardened veterans like Burke and Van Fleet took the accident in stride, the young pilot was horrified, not only by his own narrow escape but by the thought that he had almost killed two flag officers. Appreciating the fact that the pilot was shaken, both officers offered to share some ice cream with him. Without a helicopter, Burke decided to return Van Fleet to shore in the ship's landing boat. When he found that no one in the boat crew knew how to handle the boat in heavy seas, he decided to do it himself. Reassuring Van Fleet that, above all, he was a sailor, he told the fighting general that he was about to see a very unusual sight—an admiral bringing in a landing boat. The boat made it through the foaming waves safely as it thrust its bow into the sand. Both Burke and Van Fleet waded ashore. With some admiration, Burke watched as the general drove away in a jeep that had been waiting for him. (13)

In early June 1951 the *USS Los Angeles* and two destroyers positioned themselves off the bombline near Kosong. The group designated as Task Element–95.28 was comprised of the *LA,* the *USS Rush* (DD–714) and the Canadian destroyer *HMCS Nootka.* Assisted by an army spotting plane, the *Los Angeles* fired at heavy, enemy troop concentrations and received plaudits from the pilot who said, "You do a wonderful job here. Your [*Los Angeles'* and *Rush's*] firing was between strikes and this...kept the [Chinese] down for a succeeding strike."

LGEN James A. Van Fleet confers with RADM Arleigh A. Burke aboard the cruiser Los Angeles *off the coast of Korea, July 8, 1951.* U.S. NAVY

Ground forces were pleased as well when *Los Angeles*' firing had stopped a big night attack. Between strikes, the *Los Angeles* managed also to complete a SAR mission, picking up a Marine pilot with the *LA's* helicopter. (14)

Mine sweeps for safe passage were ordered as the battleship *USS New Jersey* (BB–62) joined the fray on the bombline, and the shelling continued. In the morning the *Los Angeles* was again called to break up another enemy troop concentration. Incoming reports stated that the cruiser had made "short work of it."

While the *LA* was replenishing alongside the *USS Oberon* (AKA–14), another urgent call came in from the Korean Military Advisory Group (KMAG), asking for 8–inch fire to deal with an enemy troop concentration marshaling in the town of Sindaeri. Admiral Burke decided to do both jobs. He would take on the ammunition and fire it at the same time. Without a minute to lose, crews began loading 8–inch ammunition onto one side of the cruiser only to have it unloaded "through the gun muzzles on the other side." Though observing all safety precautions in this dangerous situation, the *Los Angeles* was later asked to abstain from answering other requests until all the ammunition was fully loaded on the ship. Nonetheless, in this case, Burke's decision was the right one. *Los Angeles'* 8–inch fire had routed the communists and allowed US Army troops to advance to new positions. (15)

Rear Admiral Burke was ordered to serve on the UN negotiating team at Kaesong when the demarcation line at the 38th parallel was agreed upon on July 26, 1951. Air and naval forces continued their blockade and interdiction efforts while ground action slowed down to a "wait and see " impasse.

The *Los Angeles* left the Sea of Japan and moved to the west coast of Korea to bombard enemy positions at Haeju Man on the Onglin peninsula. The operation became known as the Han River Demonstration (See map, p. 24). The aim of this mission was to clarify an ambiguous aspect of the 38th parallel demarcation line then being negotiated. The UN command thought it critical to the interests of South Korea that it demonstrate its control over a 200–square mile area of the Onglin

A HO3C *helicopter prepares to land on the* Los Angeles *with an American soldier in need of emergency medical attention, September 12, 1951.* U.S. NAVY

peninsula west of Imjin River. The remainder of the peninsula contiguous to this vital region was held by the communists who claimed they controlled all of it. This southern section of the peninsula was of strategic importance to the Republic of South Korea because it was located near the head waters of the Han River. Because the entrance to Han River controlled the maritime approaches to the South Korean capital Seoul, it was imperative that this area not be under communist control in any armistice agreement. Moreover Haeju and the Haeju Man not only made up an important transportation link to Yonan, the area was said to be "the most popular fishing ground of South Korea." (16)

The UN command chose to use naval power to show that this area was in United Nations' hands, even though South Korean guerrillas were well established there. A truly multinational naval force participated in this joint venture. A British frigate carefully surveyed the channel while the United States Navy supplied anchors, buoys and tugs for the operation. Commonwealth frigates silenced enemy guns on the north-

USS LOS ANGELES (CA-135)

AS OUTFITTED FEBRUARY 1961
Rendering by Paul Bender

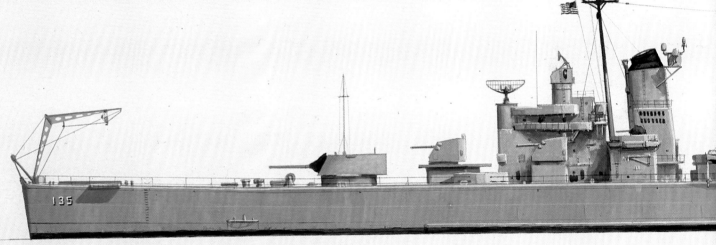

ern shore. On July 28, 1951, the *USS Los Angeles,* guided by U.S. minesweepers, entered the swept Haeju Man channel and began bombarding enemy front line positions. The enemy was caught by surprise. Apparently they did not believe that so large ship would be able to move so far up the channel. Though the heavy cruiser's gunners were privy to good intelligence concerning targets in Haeju Man, they could fire only a certain number of shots because of limited anchorage grounds. Nonetheless 48 rounds of 8–inch and six rounds of 5–inch projectiles were expended on enemy targets. The *Los Angeles* received a "well done" for her work, and the isolated peninsula west of the Imjin river was eventually acknowledged as being under South Korean rule in November 1951. Relieved by the *H.M.S. Ceylon* on July 29, the *Los Angeles* was ordered back to Task Force 77 on the east coast. (17)

The night of November 21, 1951, proved to be one of the most significant of the war on the east coast for the *LA*. The heavy cruiser had been escorting aircraft carriers of Task Force 77 at the time. Though a Russian air attack on the task force was always possible with jet bombers based nearby in Manchuria, it had not happened. The *Los Angeles'* anti-aircraft defense was an important part of the cruiser's escort duty with Task Force 77. Vice Admiral J.J. "Jocko" Clark, the commander of the task force, had to decide after an urgent message came across the wire that the North Koreans had broken through UN lines at Kojo and that ROK forces had run out of ammunition and were in dire need of help. Nearby destroyers did not have guns with sufficient range to blunt the attack. In desperation, shore spotters radioed for a "Charlie Able" (heavy cruiser) or at least another "Dog

Dog" (destroyer) for help. The only heavy ship available was the *Los Angeles*. Clark's staff insisted that the *Los Angeles* not leave its antiaircraft duties, but Clark disregarded their counsel and sent the heavy cruiser to turn back the enemy attack. The *LA* arrived off the target area half an hour before midnight. With sound intelligence reports, a barrage of her 8–inch guns turned the tide of battle. The ship's crockery rattled as the 260–pound shells hurled over the mountains and cut off communist reinforcements. This action of the *Los Angeles* helped the ROK force hold its positions and wait for reinforcements to arrive. According to Clark, "It was a question of using a ship where she could do some good." (18) Soon after the *LA* responded to a call from the nearby First Marine Division to take out enemy bunkers protected by 15 feet of earth and logs, too thick for Marine artillery. Using armor–piercing shells, the *LA's* guns blasted their way into the bunkers.

On a lighter note, a few weeks later, Ensign George E. Tompson, a native Angeleno born in the San Fernando Valley,

USS Los Angeles *screens the carrier* USS Boxer *(CV–21) in Korean waters, August 25, 1951.* U.S. NAVY

was plucked out of the Sea of Japan by the *LA's* helicopter after his fighter plane was shot down by enemy fire. He had been in the water for only a minute. Dazed and freezing, the pilot's first words after being hauled aboard the cruiser were, "Sure didn't expect to get back to Los Angeles this quick." (19)

After serving over seven months in the war zone, the heavy cruiser proudly returned to its home port on December 18, 1951. According to the *Los Angeles Times*, "Our cruiser came home yesterday," and the mileage chalked on its signal bridge showed "the *Los Angeles* [had] cruised 48,782 miles." The veteran warship was welcomed by a throng of 2,000 people as she warped into Berth 90 in San Pedro. Earlier a Navy launch had carried Los Angeles Mayor Fletcher Bowron and other civic dignitaries to meet the cruiser outside the harbor's breakwater. Included in this entourage was the leader of the bond drive which had netted over $80,000,000 for the ship's construction and the head of the Mayor's *USS Los Angeles* committee. Bowron told those gathered at the dock that the southland "is deeply proud" of the cruiser's record. He then pronounced members of the crew "honorary and honored citizens of Los Angeles." (20)

While stateside, a minor political flap concerning the cruiser broke out over the question of the warship's silver service set. It was naval custom that a silver service set for official occasions be presented by the city or state after which the ship was named. In a snafu in 1943, city officials of Los Angeles never got around to purchasing a silver set for the cruiser during the building of the ship named in its honor. It was revealed in preparing for a solemn occasion aboard the ship that its silver set bore the seal of the city of San Francisco! It had been borrowed from the heavy cruiser *USS San Francisco* (CA–38) when she was decommissioned. Some Angelenos were indignant that such a thing could happen; some said it was shameful. To eradicate the notion that this cruiser would have a rival's name in place during formal commemorations, the Alberto Lodge of the Sons of Italy pledged $100 as a starter for public funds to pay for a silver set. Nine thousand dollars was collected, but the set desired by the mayor cost $15,000. Two city councilmen bottled up the mayor's motion for using public money to make up the difference. They felt a $9,000 set was good enough. One of the councilmen, a former naval officer, said, "The set is only used for formal receptions and 99 per cent of the time is stored away in a closet." (21) The mayor won his skirmish with the City Council, however, and on September 11, 1952, Mayor Fletcher Bowron presented a 57–piece silver service from the City of Los Angeles to the warship that bore its name. (22)

The cruiser certainly deserved all the praise and recognition it received from local politicians and citizens. She had participated in 109 bombardment missions off the coast of Korea. Her 8– and 5–inch guns had poured "some 8,000 rounds of projectiles" into enemy positions. Six thousand of the enemy were killed as the ship worked to smash the communist transportation system. Moreover the cruiser's medical staff treated 43 UN personnel who were either sick or injured and rescued five "ditched" aviators during her seven–month deployment.

Over 500 members of the crew were given leave right after docking. Another 500 were invited to the Gold Room of Los Angeles' famous Ambassador Hotel for entertainment sponsored

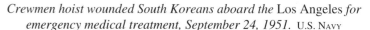

Crewmen hoist wounded South Koreans aboard the Los Angeles *for emergency medical treatment, September 24, 1951.* U.S. NAVY

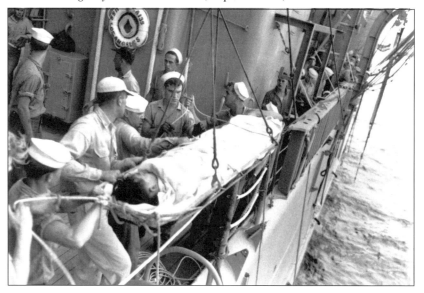

The USS Los Angeles *docks at Pier 90 in San Pedro, December 18, 1951, after returning from her first deployment to Korea.* SAN PEDRO HISTORICAL SOCIETY

by the Mayor's Cruiser Committee and the Navy League. Many of the returnees were reservists who qualified for discharge from the Navy.

The USS Los Angeles was scheduled to remain in San Pedro until after the first of the year, then go to Mare Island Naval Shipyard for an overhaul. (23) In early 1952 the heavy cruiser was repaired and fit with improved rapid firing, 3–inch, 50–cal., antiaircraft guns with advanced, fire–control directors. After a period of training off the California coast, the Los Angeles returned to the east coast of Korea on October 9, 1952, for her second deployment.

The situation in Korea had not changed greatly since the heavy cruiser had operated in Korean waters in December 1951. The so–called Sitzkrieg (sitting war) was still in place as the negotiations dragged on. The front lines became largely static, much like World War I. The truce line remained roughly the same with each side doing little more than trying to gain more high ground. It was, nonetheless, a bloody imbroglio. Twelve thousand, three hundred Americans and countless communist troops were to die during the next two–year period. The peace process was held up by prisoner exchange issues, location of the final demarcation line, and how an armistice would be enforced.

In the interim the blockade and interdiction of the North Korean coast was still in place. Breaking down the communist's logistical effort was now a harder task, however, because fewer supplies had to be sent to support troops in a stabilized battle front. Moreover the communists had over 20,000 men to repair bombed–out roads, bridges and railroad tracks. The rapidity of some of their work was illustrated by the repair of one stretch of track near Wonsan, 400 feet of which was destroyed on April 4, 1952, yet was in operation the next day. (24)

Back in the Far East, the USS Los Angeles stopped first in Yokosuka, Japan, a major naval transshipment and repair base, before returning to the Korean bombline. Accompanied by the USS John R. Craig (DD–885), the heavy cruiser made an auspicious return to the fighting front near Kosong Myon on October 11, 1952. With the destroyer Craig screening seaward, the

Captain Lawrence R. Daspit, Commanding Officer of the Los Angeles during the ship's second deployment, October 1952 to April 1953. He received the Legion of Merit for his steadfast service during the Siege of Wonsan harbor.
HARVEY M. BEIGEL COLLECTION

Los Angeles fired her main 8–inch batteries on enemy positions late in the day. Employing Shore Fire Support Parties (SFCP) to spot, the heavy cruiser shot up enemy bunkers, observation posts and trench lines. The results were impressive. SFCP and air spotters reported that seven bunkers had been destroyed, nine damaged, an observation post destroyed, and 100 yards of trench line damaged. Five gun positions and supply buildings had also been taken under fire. That night the enemy was subjected to H and I (harassing and interdiction) fire on 16 targets along the bombline.

The next day LA's gun fire disrupted road traffic. October 13 saw the heavy cruiser fire in support of the I ROK Corp's Fifth Division; her 5–inch guns silenced a 76–mm enemy gun. The cruiser's main batteries fired at two enemy 120–mm guns and bunkers with some success. During periods of calm, the crew heard the sounds of firing on the beach. "Men on the deck found it thrillingly frightening to watch the flashes as artillery duels lighted the inky sky and tracer shells rose in a screaming arc of fire, then fell to earth with a deadly thud." (25) After a few days of daytime and night firing, the *Los Angeles* and escort were relieved by the *USS Helena* (CA–73) task element.

While enemy counterfire along the coast doubled in volume from July 1952 to January 1953, it had not yet reached the intensity of the last few months of the war. Further complicating operations was the severe Korean weather. A writer on the *USS Los Angeles* noted:

The ship spent the first week in December on the Bombline. A blizzard, the first heavy snow of the year, began the morning of the 2nd and continued most of the day, covering the ship with a blanket of snow several inches deep. Winter had come to Korea. Men in exposed positions found that even heavy foul weather clothing couldn't keep out the bitter chill of the sharp, biting winds which swept out of Siberia and across the bleak and jagged mountains of Korea to whip snow and freezing salt spray across the decks as the ship was lifted and tossed in the raging confusion of dark, angry seas. The clammy cold even penetrated below decks. The men cursed the cold, pulled on extra sweaters, shivered, and went on about the business of delivering concentrated death to the enemy. (26)

During this time, the *Los Angeles* and other heavy ships operated in a predictable pattern. For example the *Los Angeles* bombarded Songjin (Cobra Patrol) in the north and then joined the aircraft carriers of Task Force 77 as an escort. The heavy cruiser with destroyer screen also gave artillery support on a number of occasions to both the I ROK Corps and X U.S. Army Corps on the bombline. Less predictable were the SAR (sea and air rescue) missions. One such unusual case occurred later off Wonsan on March 4, 1953, when a spot plane was hit by enemy antiaircraft fire. When the pilot survived a malfunctioning parachute jump and was "swinging like a pendulum" from the *LA's* helicopter which had been sent to pick him up, nearby enemy troops left their positions and began firing on both him and the helicopter. In response, the heavy cruiser fired a heavy 5–inch gun barrage at these enemy troops who had come out in the open to capture the pilot. Ten of the enemy were killed. The *LA's* helicopter pilot Ensign Lester B. Shackford was later awarded the Distinguished Flying Cross for bringing the severely burned Navy pilot back to the heavy cruiser. (27)

Another factor commonplace to operations on the Korean east Coast was the pattern of relief by one Task Element for another, usually after four or five days of duty. After disengagement the *LA* would be replenished. By the time the *LA* had first arrived in Korea, mobile logistic support operations had already been reestablished. With the constancy of the fire support and interdiction missions of carriers and other surface vessels requiring resupply at sea, it was not uncommon to see oilers, ammunition ships and store ships alongside the *Los Angeles* and other ships. Thus at least one battle group or task force could remain on station on the bombline and siege operations at all times; this avoided the wasteful 1,600– or 1,700– mile round trip to Japan for resupply. By 1952 an entire task force could be replenished in ten to twelve hours. According to one authority, the success of the at–sea, logistic support effort

---

Working the decks on the cruiser Los Angeles *in Korean waters.*

"was one of the unheralded achievements of the Korean War." (28)

During the six–month deployment to Korea, there were a few jaunts to Yokosuka, Japan, for repairs, and once the *LA* sailed to Hong Kong for R&R where, among other things, the crew hosted a Christmas party for orphans. Finally the *Los Angeles,* like other siege ships, engaged the enemy at his most heavily defended stronghold Wonsan Harbor. Operations there occurred in conjunction with the shelling of enemy bombline positions or an attack up the coast to Songjin.

The bombardment of Wonsan harbor was no easy task. The siege of this North Korean railroad center, midway between Vladivostok and Pusan, had entered its third year. From November 1952 to April 1953 the *Los Angeles* participated in 11 siege operations and was fired upon on five separate occasions. The port lay in rugged terrain; there were steep-sided islands in the bay which were green in the summer and snow speckled in the winter. Some of the islands were under UN control and furnished gun spot and intelligence information; others were held by the communists and were used in counter–battery fire. The harbor was heavily mined, and UN ships had to operate

The Los Angeles *brings happiness to Korean orphans, October 1951.* U.S. NAVY

in swept areas. Communist batteries were trained on the intruding UN ships, UN–held islands and potential amphibious landing sites. There were 76–mm guns in the nearby hills and large 122–mm and 155–mm guns located farther from the beach. Tank and rail mounted guns were ready for use as well. Cruisers and battleships could fire at the larger, more distant guns, while destroyers entered the swept areas and fired at closer, shore gun positions. Some destroyers were on station in Wonsan for as long as two weeks. In fact "Destroyers still hold Wonsan" was a familiar line in reports to task force commanders during the siege. (29)

Persistent UN air–gun attacks marred the beautiful landscape of Wonsan and left the smell of acrid, smokeless powder in the harbor. While carrier aircraft pounded the city incessantly, mine sweepers expanded the swept areas where destroyers and heavier ships could fire at targets. Two sweepers were sunk, some of the siege ships were hit, and it was not uncommon for ships to enter Wonsan harbor with fresh war color and leave with paint scorched by muzzle blast. (30)

Crewmen might ask themselves, "What are we gaining in this endless siege?" Enemy cave guns on Kalma Gak, an arm of land which extended out into the bay, continued to be a problem. In truth the long siege did force the communists to keep several North Korean divisions near the city for fear that the constant shelling might be a prelude to an amphibious assault. Moreover control over the sea approaches to the city decreased the importance of this "Chicago" of the North and made UN ascendancy there helpful at the bargaining table at Panmunjom.

In early January 1953 the defenders of Wonsan stepped up their campaign against the siege ships. A record number of shells began raining on United States ships. The sinking of an American battleship or cruiser would have been a colossal propaganda victory for the communists. Coming from well–camouflaged cave guns on shore, the increased counterfire was more accurate, and communist gunners were able to get hits with fewer rounds.

Turret III blasting a two-gun salvo at enemy positions near Suwan Dan, North Korea. Note the two projectiles in the air. HARVEY M. BEIGEL COLLECTION

The *USS Los Angeles* entered Wonsan harbor approximately a dozen times during her second deployment between November 24, 1952, and April 13, 1953. The *LA* had returned from Yokusuka, Japan, on November 19, 1952, by way of Shimonoseki Straits. There she was met by the *USS Lyman K. Swensen* (DD–769), forming Task Element 77.17 under the command of Captain Lawrence R. Daspit, USN, Commanding Officer of the *LA*. After spending several days on the bombline, the Task Unit went north on November 24, 1952, for a gun strike at Wonsan harbor some fifty miles up the coast, but poor weather prevented any action. With visibility clearing later in the day, the SFCP directed the cruiser's gunfire at a tank cave. The tank was set on fire, and the cave was damaged by accurately fired projectiles. The *Los Angeles* was the first ship to hit this target, this after 1,500 rounds had been expended on it by a number of other ships. Damage to bunker and coastal defense guns could not be assessed because of weather conditions. The 5–inch batteries, however, fired at exposed enemy troops on the beach. TE 77.17 left Wonsan at 1600 and returned to the bombline. (31)

Enemy shells bursting around the Los Angeles *in Wonsan Harbor during a March 27, 1953, gun strike.* HARVEY M. BEIGEL COLLECTION

An 8–inch gun salvo fired from Turret I. HARVEY M. BEIGEL COLLECTION

Shrapnel holes in the after–stack as a result of an April 2 hit on the cruiser's mainmast. HARVEY M. BEIGEL COLLECTION

A hole in the mainmast where an enemy shell burst during an April 2, 1953 gun strike at Wonsan Harbor targets. HARVEY M. BEIGEL COLLECTION

The heavy cruiser's next visit to Wonsan was on December 5 when she and the *USS Philip* (DDE–498) entered the harbor before noon. For approximately two hours, the *Los Angeles* focused her main batteries on a railroad marshaling yard, an ammunition storage area and an underground facility, all with good results. At the same time the cruiser, using ship spot, hit an enemy mortar company's billet area and bunker. After putting observers ashore, the two ships returned to the bombline. (32)

Heavy snowfall canceled a half–day attack on Wonsan planned for January 7, 1953, but the *Los Angeles* and the *USS James E. Kyes* (DD–787) arrived at firing positions the next day. Utilizing SFCP and air spot, the cruiser hit enemy gun targets and enemy buildings, despite unusually poor weather. Better results were obtained the next week when the *LA* lobbed her 8–inch projectiles, making a direct hit on a gun port. During a four and a half–hour period, the cruiser destroyed six buildings and a heavy mortar position with the help of Marine SFCP spots. The *Los Angeles'* own guns malfunctioned at Wonsan during this period, and gunners were forced to fire only directly ahead and astern. After completing more coastal patrols and

Three–inch guns fire. HARVEY M. BEIGEL COLLECTION

bombline missions, the heavy cruiser headed for Yokosuka, Japan, on January 27 for a scheduled rest and upkeep period. (33)

When the *USS Los Angeles* returned to Korea, she rendezvoused with Task Force 77 and served as an antiaircraft support ship with the carrier force for two weeks. After a short stint on the bombline, the cruiser once again headed for Wonsan on February 28 for a heavy gun strike. Her main and secondary batteries commenced fire at 0900. The results of this four-hour siege operation were rewarding. Nineteen buildings were destroyed with heavy damage to several more buildings and hits on gun area positions. Again on March 4, the cruiser's gunners went after targets in Wonsan. They made four, main battery direct hits on two coastal guns and other hits on an explosive storage area and enemy billets. While TF 77 air spotters adjusted 5–inch fire on a supply area target, a 3–inch battery inflicted damage on a gun position. Those guns unfortunately had reliability problems during much of the second tour. Three out of the eight mounts experienced short circuits and were put out of action. Even more troubling was the fact that with a maximum range of 30,000 feet, the 3–inchers were inadequate against enemy jets with nuclear weapons. Even though the guns had a rate of fire of about fifty rounds per minute, their accuracy was only marginal. Moreover the gun suffered from bore erosion and a consequent decrease in barrel life. (34) After night bombardment on the bombline, the *Los Angeles* left for Yokosuka, Japan, for leave and upkeep. (36)

About three weeks later on March 22, both the *Los Angeles* and the battleship *Missouri* (BB–63) conducted more gun strikes in Wonsan harbor. The big ships were responding to an increase of enemy activity which seemed bent on destroying UN minesweeping capability and retaking UN–held harbor islands. Communist shore batteries opened fire on the *Los Angeles* with one surface and two air bursts exploding near the cruiser. No hits were made, however. Using air spot from TF 77 planes, the *Los Angeles* scored several direct hits on railroad bridge approaches and one railway tunnel. Also damaged were a bridge repair facility and a highway bridge. The strike ended in less

than three hours when the cruiser returned to the bombline in the company of *USS Hamner* (DD–718). (37)

March 27 was an eventful day for the *Los Angeles* in Wonsan Harbor. The cruiser was taken under fire by very accurate shore batteries with seemingly unlimited ammunition. The ship began evasive action by shooting at cave gun positions which were attacking the UN–held island of Hwangto Do. When the enemy ceased fire, the ship proceeded to a swept area designated "Muffler" and continued firing at gun positions until she reached the end of the safe area; then she reversed course. At this point, enemy fire from a different area broke out, and the *Los Angeles* reversed course again and moved back toward "Muffler," firing at the newly revealed enemy positions. Sixty splashes were observed near the *LA*. The rounds fell from 25 feet to a 1,000 yards from the ship. One of the 76–mm rounds hit the cruiser. The shell exploded outside a Mk 35 radar control room amidships, tearing a gaping hole in the steel overhead and hurling shrapnel over a wide area. The ship's crew quickly repaired a damaged 3–inch mount. Luckily there were no casualties. (36)

The *USS Los Angeles* was not the only ship hit in the spring of 1953 as the communists tried to end the naval siege of Wonsan. In April the *USS Maddox* (DD–731) took a hit from a 76–mm shell on the 16th; the *USS James E. Kyes* (DD–787) was also struck on the 19th. Both ships suffered casualties.(38)

On April 2, 1953, the *Los Angeles* was hit by a 105–mm projectile. The *Los Angeles* had entered Wonsan Harbor at dawn to deliver the Commander of Cruiser Division Five Rear Admiral William V. O'Regan and a Marine general to Yodo Island for an inspection. The *LA* then moved closer to her targets and fired her main batteries at a supply building, damaging it heavily. The cruiser then fired at three cave gun positions making several hits in each cave. The 5– and 3–inch guns added their fire on newly activated gun positions with several hits on cave entrances being observed. The destroyer *Hamner* took on enemy positions as well and, though straddled by 30 splashes, was not hit. The *Los Angeles* was not spared, however, and took a hit. The projectile dented the heavily armored ship's main mast. Shrapnel from the explosion ripped large jagged holes

Above are the twelve recipients awarded Purple Hearts for wounds received from the enemy hit, April 2. HARVEY M. BEIGEL COLLECTION

in the plating of the nearby superstructure. A total of 18 men in two open gun mounts received shrapnel wounds, only 12 of whom required medical treatment. None of the wounds was of a serious nature. Fourteen other crew members were hit by shrapnel which was deflected by armored vests. The performance of the crew was reported "outstanding." Naval records show that, "Although some personnel fatigue was noticeable under the pressure of daily firing over a long period of time along with dawn and dusk alerts, performance of most personnel continued at a high level of efficiency." (39)

Resolutely, the *USS Los Angeles* returned to the besieged harbor at Wonsan two more times before she finished her second Korean tour. Between visits to the siege area, the cruiser worked along the bombline and patrolled in support of UN forces on Nando Do, a UN island base on the 39th parallel. The *Los Angeles* returned to Wonsan on April 7 and 14 and did a lot of damage. TF 77 air spotters reported that the heavy cruiser did "excellent shooting" there. The cruiser's guns destroyed enemy gun positions and buildings and made two direct hits on a concrete pill box. Her 8–inch batteries closed one cave

while secondary guns scored a direct hit on an antiaircraft battery. Later in the day, two rounds of large–caliber shells were fired at the cruiser, but the closest round fell 1,000 yards astern. Operating with *USS Eversole* (DD–789) the next week, the two ships caused similar damage to the North Korean logistic system in Wonsan. One enemy round was fired at the two ships but landed approximately 2,000 yards away. (40)

The *USS Los Angeles* took part in 31 consecutive days of shore bombardment and UN troop support during this period. This was said to be the longest bombardment by a single ship in naval history. It was, therefore, great relief to the crew when the *LA* served its last five days in Korea as the heavy support ship for the Task Force 77 carrier group. On April 22, Vice Admiral J.J. Clark, Commander of the 7th Fleet, came aboard the *LA* to present awards to the officers and men of the heavy cruiser and the staff of Commander Cruiser Five (Comcrudiv 5) for their outstanding "accomplishments during the present tour." Among the decorations was the Legion of Merit presented to Captain Lawrence R. Daspit, *LA's* Commanding Officer, already a recipient of the Navy Cross. Twelve young enlisted men received Purple Hearts as a result of wounds received April 2 when the ship was hit at Wonsan. On April 23 the *LA* arrived in Yokosuka for onward routing to her home port on the west coast. (41)

The cruiser arrived in Long Beach, California, on May 15, 1953, to a tumultuous welcome. The warship's performance in Korea had been outstanding. On the seven–month tour of duty off the war–torn peninsula, the *Los Angeles* had fired nearly 17,000 rounds of ammunition and according to observers, killed or wounded 53 enemy personnel. She had also been a target of enemy shore guns on five separate occasions and had been hit twice. As the *Los Angeles Times* put it, the battle–scarred veteran cruiser *"USS Los Angeles* was home again from the war." (42) Over 2,000 friends and loved ones, a sixty–piece military band and a beauty queen awaited the 1,300 veterans as the cruiser approached Municipal Pier B in Long Beach. According to the *Los Angeles Times*, "Eagerness" to get home may have been the reason why the cruiser "slipped a little too far forward in her tight berth and nudged the wooden pier ahead" upon docking. Whatever the cause of this minor mishap, it was a joyous reunion for everybody, and most of the crew had a thirty–day leave to look forward to. (43) The arrival of the *LA* in Long Beach was especially promising for one sailor from New Mexico. He was unexpectedly met at the dock by two young women— "pen pals" he had been introduced to through the Los Angeles Chamber of Commerce. He had written to them during the Korean tour. Determined to see their "lonesome sailor," the two attractive ladies took the young man in "tow for dancing and a tour of the city" and picked up the tab. (44)

Another event involving crew members of the *USS Los Angeles* and a young lady was less promising. On July 16, 1953, two of the *LA's* enlisted men were in the ship's brig facing trial and possible court–martial for smuggling an eighteen–year old waitress aboard the ship. The expected charge was "conduct to the prejudice of good order and discipline," and the penalty would probably be a loss of pay and hard labor at a detention barracks. The two were "restricted" on board as the ship went to sea on a training exercise sixty miles off the coast. (45) The girl "stowaway," a resident of Long Beach, was sent to the Los Angeles County Jail under a $1,000 bond. The charge was "illegally wearing a Navy uniform." She explained to federal officials that she had wanted to go aboard ship to see her ex–husband, a member of the crew. She said she had met some sailors at a bar and bet them that she could get aboard the *LA*. At first, the sailors laughed at her; then two of them decided to help her. One sailor gave her a pair of blues and a cap; the other gave her an identification card. Seeing that her hair would not pass inspection, they took her behind the building behind the Navy Landing and cropped off her hair. After teaching her to say, "Permission to come aboard, Sir," they took a liberty boat out to the ship. Once on the ship—the officer of the deck had failed to notice anything strange about her appearance— she went to a sailor's bunk. He covered her with blankets, and at about 6:30 A.M. he brought her some breakfast. She became alarmed, however, when he told her that there was talk about a woman being aboard. When guns began to roar in a

practice exercise, she unwittingly jumped into a fire control radar room, disregarding a sign on the door which read, "Danger High Voltage. Do Not Enter." At this point, Shore Patrol men entered the room. One of them angrily told her, "Sister, we're...going to hang you from the highest yardarm on the ship," and took her to the Master of Arms shack.

The response to the incident was varied. One newspaper reported that, "The official silence was deafening." (46) On the other hand, a Federal Commissioner examining the case was quoted as saying, "You know, this is a rather peculiar situation—most unusual, you know." (47) While one Navy source cautiously admitted that the case was "a once in–the–life–time incident—humorous in some respects," a spokesman for the Commander Cruisers and Destroyers of the Pacific Fleet said the prank had a serious side with two enlisted men confined aboard ship pending an investigation. With volunteer counsel, one of whom was a former Navy legal officer, the young woman was released to take a waitress job in a Los Angeles Cafe owned by an ex–Navy man. Because of changes in the US Attorney's Office, future action on her misdemeanor charge was uncertain. (48)

"Always room for another warrior." Senior Medical Officer James G. Seyfried aids an Essex *pilot who had been plucked from the water by the* LA's *helicopter after he crash–landed his damaged plane astern of the cruiser on December 9, 1952.*

END NOTES

(1) *Los Angeles Examiner,* December 5, 1950, *Dictionary of the American Naval Fighting Ships* (Washington: Naval History Division) Vol. IV, p. 144.

(2) Dean Allard, "An Era of Transition, 1945–1953," in Kenneth J. Hagan, *In Peace and War: Interpretations of American Naval History,* 1775–1984 (Westport: Greenwood Press, 1984), p. 296.

(3) Malcolm Muir, Jr., *Black Shoes and Blue Water: Surface Warfare in the United States Navy, 1945–1975* (Washington: Naval Historical Center, 1996), p. 14.

(4) Stephen Terzibaschitsch, *Cruisers of the U.S. Navy, 1922–1962* (Annapolis: U.S. Naval Institute Press, 1984), p. 220.

(5) *Long Beach Press–Telegram,* April 14, 1951.

(6) Kim Sang Mo, "The Implications of the Sea War in Korea," *Naval War College Review* (Summer 1967), p. 126.

(7) Malcom W. Cagle and Frank A. Manson, *The Sea War in Korea* (Annapolis: U.S. Naval Institute Press, 1957), p. 283.

(8) Sheldon Kinney, "All Quiet at Wonsan," *United States Institute Proceedings,* August, 1954, p. 859.

(9) Quoted in E.B. Potter, *Admiral Arleigh Burke: A Biography* (New York: Random House, 1990), p. 353.

(10) Quoted in Paik Sun Yup, *From Pusan to Panmunjom* (Washington: Brassey's [US], Inc.), p. 160.

(11) E.B. Potter, op. cit., p. 354.

(12) *Ibid.*

(13) *Ibid.,* p. 356.

(14) *Commander Cruiser Divison Five, War Diary,* June 1–30, 1951, pp. 10–15.

(15) *Ibid.,* p. 15. *Los Angeles Examiner*, June 11, 1951.

(16) *War Diary,* July 26, 1951, p. 13.

(17) *Ibid,* p. 14.

(18) Admiral J.J. Clark (Retired), *Carrier Admiral* (New York: David McKay Company, 1967), pp. 279–80.

(19) *Los Angeles Examiner,* December 9, 1951.

(20) *Long Beach Press–Telegram,* December 18, 1951.

(21) *Los Angeles Examiner,* May 6, 1952.

(22) *Ibid.,* September 12, 1952.

(23) *Los Angeles Times,* December 18, 1951.

(24) Cagle and Manson, op. cit., p. 271.

(25) *Action Report: USS Los Angeles* Serial 050, 13 November 1952, Enclosure (2), p. 7. *The Cruise of the* USS Los Angeles, *1952–1953, Cruise Book,* p. 17.

(26) *Cruise Book, Ibid.,* p. 19.

(27) *Action Report:* Serial 058, 11 March 1953, Enclosure (1), pp. 2–3. Memo from Donald J. Dessart to the Director of the Los Angeles Maritime Museum, August 28, 1996.

(28) Thomas Wildenburg, *Gray and Steel and Black Oil: Fast Tankers and Replenishment at Sea in the U.S. Navy, 1912–1955* (Annapolis: U.S. Naval Institute Press, 1996), p. 219.

(29) Richard B. Phillip, "The Siege of Wonsan," *Army Information Digest,* November, 1953, p. 44.

(30) Sheldon Kinney, op. cit., p. 860.

(31) *Action Report:* Serial 063. 30 December 1952, Enclosure (1), p. 2.
(32) *Action Report:* Serial 063. 30 December 1952, Enclosure (3), p. 1.
(33) *Action Report:* Serial 033. 29 January 1953, Enclosure (1), p. 3.
(34) *Action Report:* "East Coast of Korea," 21 Nov.–17Dec. 1952.
(35) *Action Report:* Serial 058, 11 March 1953, Enclosure (1), p. 2.
(36) *Action Report:* Serial 071, 27 April 1953, Enclosure (1), p. 4.
(37) *Ibid., p. 5–6.*
(38) Cagle and Manson, op. cit., p. 437.
(39) *Action Report:* Serial 071, 27 April 1953, Enclosure (1), p. 13.
(40) *Ibid., p. 6–8.*
(41) *Ibid., p. 11.*
(42) *Los Angeles Times,* May 16, 1953.
(43) *Ibid.*
(44) The *Sea Hawk,* June 1953, Vol. 3 No. 5, p.1.
(45) *Los Angeles Examiner,* July 16, 1953.
(46) *Ibid.,* July 15, 1953.
(47) *Los Angeles Times,* July 15, 1953.
(48) *Ibid.,* July 17, 1953.

The USS Los Angeles *at anchor off the coast of Korea after shelling enemy installations in North Korea, July 4, 1951.* U.S. Navy

The USS Los Angeles *sailing off the California coast, n.d.*
SAN PEDRO ELKS CLUB

WESTPAC

Between November 1953 and June 1963, the *USS Los Angeles* made eight deployments to the Far East from her home port of Long Beach, California. Sailing mainly along the Pacific rim, known to Navy men as WestPac—short for Western Pacific—the *LA* had patrolled these unstable seas since the end of World War II. American warships showed the stars and stripes in such places as Manila, Singapore, Bangkok and Saigon. Along with being a highly visible emblem of American power, the ships of the 7th Fleet performed many varied missions in the Far East. They rescued American citizens or friendly foreign nationals or enforced quarantines or escorted distressed merchant men. In an era of declining colonialism, the demonstration of American power was reassuring to new regimes facing the growing wave of communist revolts. As if to dramatize American ascendancy in the region, both the cruisers *Los Angeles* and *Rochester* (CA–124) participated in Operation Flag Hoist, an amphibious exercise on the island of Iwo Jima in 1954. (1) This large operation may have been a response to the growing fear that the West was being outflanked and isolated by some Asian nations that were seemingly moving towards communism. With the expansion of nationalism and communism in the Pacific rim, it was felt that certain "choke points" like Tsushima Strait or the Strait of Malacca or even the Taiwan Straits were at

risk of falling into communist hands. These losses would deny the West its strategic position in the region and with that the loss of the fabled Asian trade.

The premier task of the 7th Fleet was to deter the largest communist state in the region, the People's Republic of China, from taking aggressive military action against American and western interests. To achieve this goal, the 7th Fleet ultimately

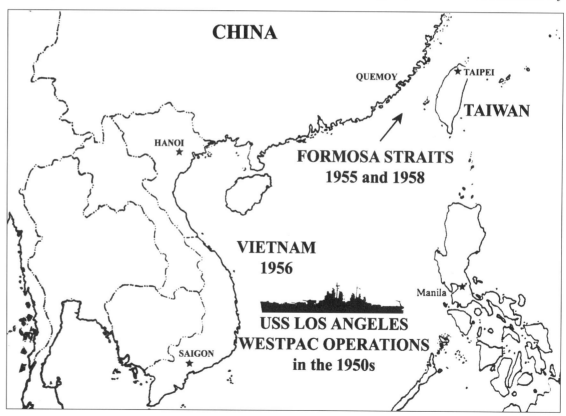

became the regional police and rapid intervention force in the Pacific. This was made possible because warships did not need local bases and airfields from which to operate in emergencies. They could stay at sea and depart at will. In the 1950s gunboat diplomacy was reborn to contain communist aggression with both an American peacetime presence and a possible crisis intervention as a deterrent. It was known among the 60,000 men of the fleet that their main function was to train to be ready for war. (2) On a day–to–day basis, much of the fleet's time was spent tracking Soviet submarines and destroyers and keeping a constant watch on Chinese coastal traffic.

Surface ships like the *USS Los Angeles* remained in service until the early 1960s. The Korean war had demonstrated that even in the atomic age, limited wars with conventional weapons were likely to occur. Looking at the record, a 1954 Naval War College study showed that the gunships of the Korean War had proved their worth and were especially useful for "precision bombardment in support of troops." Moreover weapons experimentation underway on these ships was leading to the development of the first sea–based, operational guided missiles. Four ships of the ten–year–old, *Baltimore*–class heavy cruisers were being modified to carry Regulus I missiles with tactical nuclear warheads. (3)

The *USS Los Angeles* was the first cruiser selected for a Regulus I missile conversion. Notice of this occurred when it was announced July 21, 1954, that a new guided missile launcher was being installed on the *LA* during her refit at Mare Island Naval Shipyard. The cruiser's Commanding Officer W.W. Outerbridge, though enthusiastic about the addition of guided missile capacity to the *LA,* spoke guardedly to reporters. He announced that the cruiser was the first west coast ship "capable of launching the new weapons," but he emphasized that the new armament "wouldn't change the *Los Angeles'* function as a cruiser." On October 28, 1954, the *LA* was the first ship to carry out evaluation tests deploying the Regulus I strategic cruise missile. The missile was successfully recovered after a pass over San Nicholas Island off the southern California coast. (5) Four months later, the *Los Angeles* tested the Regulus sys-

The USS Los Angeles *is shown here at the Mare Island Naval Shipyard in Vallejo, California, where she was undergoing a major overhaul which included the outfitting of an experimental guided missile launcher. She became the first west coast ship capable of firing a Regulus I guided missile, 1954.*
USC SPECIAL COLLECTIONS

tem all the way through to nuclear detonation off Hawaii. Later that year, the *Los Angeles* made the first cruiser deployment to the Far East carrying three missiles, each armed with a W–5 nuclear warhead. Eventually, three other heavy cruisers were modified to carry Regulus missiles. They were the *Helena* (CA-75), *Toledo* (CA–133) and *Macon* (CA–132). The first two and the *Los Angeles* operated with the 7th Fleet in the Pacific; the *Macon* sailed with the 6th Fleet in the Mediterranean. The missiles were targeted principally at Soviet submarine and air bases. (6)

The Regulus I missile gave heavy cruisers a new mission. The four, *Baltimore*–class cruisers were proud ships, despite the feeling among many in the Navy that they were lingering survivors of another era. (7) Along with the missile–carrying submarines and aircraft carriers equipped with Regulus I missiles, cruisers were now being readied to participate in land attacks. Flying at high subsonic speeds, the 13,484–pound missile could make vertical terminal dives on a target. It could fly at altitudes from near wave–top level up to 35,000 feet and had a range of 500 nautical miles. Patterned after the assault drones of the Korean War period, the Regulus I flew with a guidance plane. As the weapon neared the target, its escort broke away at a 45–degree angle and aligned the missile with the target while arming and detonating its warhead. (8)

Unlike submarines which carried Regulus I missiles and had to undergo modifications to build bulky and expensive new hangers for missile storage, the cruisers could easily store and maintain three missiles in large hangers aft which had been originally designed to house scout planes. The big cruisers had ample space to test equipment and store spare parts; for this reason cruisers were far more compatible with Regulus I missiles and their gear than submarines were. Regulus I Missiles tested on aircraft carriers were generally held as unsatisfactory because they interfered with standard flight operations. Because cruisers had more room than submarines could possibly ever have, ordinance specialists reported they would be able to mate the missile with the appropriate warhead while at sea. Cruisers on deterrent patrol were therefore able to respond more

flexibly to tactical situations as they occurred. A cruiser's operations officer could more readily switch from a nuclear warhead to a conventional one, depending on circumstances. (9)

The ship's main battery officer was responsible for the Regulus systems aboard the heavy cruisers. Lieutenant Robert Wertheim held that job on the *USS Los Angeles* when the Regulus I missiles were hoisted aboard ship in 1955. He was confronted with two immediate problems: the storage and security of the warheads and limiting access to the restricted missile operating area on the ship. He was constantly challenged by the ship's damage control officer who demanded access over the entire ship.

Wertheim could attest to the fact that preparation for a missile launch was a laborious job, taking up to six hours. Attaching the 1,000–pound booster was no easy task. The crew used block and tackle, "at best... a difficult and tedious operation." Moreover the first Regulus launcher on the *LA* was a jury–rigged arrangement composed of a set of rails elevated by a hydraulic lift. When sailors moved the missile out of the han-

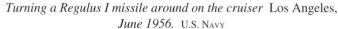

Turning a Regulus I missile around on the cruiser Los Angeles, *June 1956.* U.S. NAVY

gar and put it on the launcher, they started the missile engine and activated the lift. Wertheim recalled the scene:

Visualize...a small jet airplane up on rails that were elevated high into the air and pointing up on an angle of 35 or 40 degrees, supported by two arms extended vertically.... As the ship would roll this whole mechanism would sway back and forth, wave around in the breeze so to speak...with the jet engine whining and with the high explosive in a nuclear warhead and jato bottles ready to be ignited—the whole thing was a disaster waiting for a place to happen. (10)

This risky arrangement was soon replaced by improved equipment, and Regulus I officers were able to launch missiles at 25 knots in smooth seas. Concern over the guidance system persisted, and at times a chase plane was used to control the weapon, but even this type of guidance gave spotty results. In a wartime situation, however, Regulus I could compensate for

Firing a Regulus I missile from the cruiser Los Angeles, *August 9, 1957. The aircraft carrier* USS Ticonderoga (CV–14) *is on the right.* U.S. Navy

its lack of accuracy with its large nuclear warhead. The warhead, carrying either a W–5 nuclear warhead or a W–27 thermonuclear warhead, yielded a frightful 1.9 megatons. (11)

In June 1957 the *LA's* sister ship *Helena* (CA–75) demonstrated the potential of the Regulus I when one of her missiles flew 280 miles over the East China Sea and scored a direct hit on the target island of Okino Daito Shima; other missiles did not shoot as straight, one missing its mark by ten miles. Even with these inconsistences, cruisers began making operational patrols in 1955 with the Regulus I. The *Macon* (CA–132) operated off Egypt during the Suez crisis of 1956, and in the Pacific the *Los Angeles* and the *Helena* steamed with the 7th Fleet during the Quemoy–Matsu crises of 1955 and 1958. (12)

Yet, as is the case of other technological achievements, progress never moves in a straight line. This was true in an embarrassing occurrence on May 11, 1958, at the Commissioning Ceremonies at the new Port Arquello Naval Missile Facility north of Santa Barbara, California. With 5,000 people on hand including Senator William F. Knowland of California, a Regulus I missile was to have been launched from the fantail of the *USS Los Angeles* about a mile off shore. The cruiser had steamed north from Long Beach for this special occasion. Along with other missile firing mishaps that day, the *LA's* Regulus I firing was cancelled. The Navy later explained the failure to launch was the result of "salt water" contamination. Senator Knowland lauded the new facility as ready to launch missiles on a regular basis, as the *LA* headed back to Long Beach. One San Pedro reporter informed her readers that while no one was hurt at the demonstration, her assignment was, "Closer to being a war correspondent than I wanted to get." (13)

Cruisermen worked hard to improve and extend the performance of Regulus I in order to retain missile capability for surface ships. They envisioned missile use against ships and small shore military targets such as radar installations. They also foresaw Regulus attacks preceding air strikes in order to suppress enemy antiaircraft sites and radar installations. It was presumed that these assaults would allow carrier aircraft greater freedom to concentrate on their targets. To carry out these missions, Regulus I needed to combine great accuracy with a "fire–and–forget" method of guidance. In 1958 the Navy explored two complicated tracks to this end: inertial navigation and terrain recognition. Though difficult, these two techniques finally began to yield results in the 1970s. By 1957 Regulus I supporters were optimistic and called for a thirty–one missile cruiser force. (14)

This ambitious outcome never took place, however. The introduction of the Polaris, solid fuel, ballistic missile had two distinct advantages over the cruiser–launched, winged air–breather: it could launch underseas and had greater immunity to attack. At the same time Regulus I was not without promise. It had superior accuracy, and it could hit a greater variety of targets. Moreover Regulus I, unlike Polaris, could be redirected in flight. Several officers insisted that the Regulus cruise missiles in the Navy's inventory could undertake most strategic missions, thus making the then risky Polaris redundant.

But even the successful flights of the supersonic Regulus II could not prevent the demise of the swept wing missile. Eisenhower's tight military budget could not pay for the *Forrestal*–class super carriers, the Polaris–firing, nuclear powered submarines and the Regulus II all at the same time. When aviators saw that funding for both the Regulus II and manned naval aircraft were "coming out of the same pocket," there was no doubt that the improved Regulus II program would be left to atrophy. In 1958 the Regulus II was cut from the budget. Some weapons experts felt that this was the biggest single weapons mistake the Navy had ever made. (15)

During these same years beginning in 1950, the 7th Fleet patrolled the Formosa Straits. American presidents utilized the fleet as trip–wire for keeping the Chinese communists and the nationalists apart. This became difficult during the Korean War and later when the Chinese communists, emboldened by the French defeat in Indochina, tried to "liberate" Taiwan. That island was formerly known as Formosa. In 1955 and again in 1958 the communists tried to drive the nationalist Chinese from the offshore islands of Quemoy and Matsu, just off the coast of mainland China. Some nationalist military experts perceived the loss of the two islands as a threat to Taiwan's security. The communists, on the other hand, saw those same islands as a nuisance and a threat to the Amoy area on the mainland. The nationalists made it clear they believed those islands were absolutely essential for the defense of Taiwan.

In July 1954 Mao Tse Tung ordered bombardment of the islands. Then on January 10, 1955, the communists attacked the Tachen Islands. Though some 200 miles north of Taiwan and Quemoy and Matsu, the communist invasion of Ichiang island in the Tachen group gave impetus to the passage of the Formosa Resolution by the American congress two weeks later. This resolution gave the president the power to use American forces to defend Formosa (Taiwan) and the Pescadores Islands but was ambiguous about defending Quemoy and Matsu. Overriding appeals by Admiral Arthur W. Radford and other members of the Joint Chiefs of Staff to put troops on the offshore islands and to bomb the mainland, Eisenhower chose a different course. Believing that the Tachen Islands were indefensible and not relevant to the defense of Taiwan, he ordered the 7th Fleet to evacuate the 27,000 nationalist troops and their equipment from those northern islands. This took place February 6–13, 1955. Eisenhower's response was no "giveaway" as some critics of the action contended, because the Tachens had little relation to the defense of Formosa. Of great significance to those in Peking viewing this power play, however, was that this successful evacuation of the islands demonstrated the presence and the might of American sea power in the area. While the execution of that amphibious operation irritated the communists, it made them all the more apprehensive about what American naval power could do in the future. (16)

In early 1955 the *Los Angeles* had been perched comfortably at her Long Beach home port as the crisis broke out. On February 8 the cruiser and ten other ships were ordered immediately to Formosan waters. The crisis generated real dockside anxiety as the ships speedily departed. Emotions ran high. One 17–year–old girl broke down in tears when the ship carrying her fiance sailed without a chance for a final embrace. Her disappointment was no match, however, for that of a sailor's mother who missed seeing her son off because foggy weather delayed her trip from New Mexico. In Long Beach persistent rumors had been circulating that the *LA* had recently been "fitted for atomic armament during its recent modification." To calm this concern, the Navy announced that the *LA's* sudden departure was only a matter of a normal rotation with a similar ship type in the Formosa area. (17) The truth was that the *Los Angeles* did carry three nuclear–armed, tactical, Regulus I missiles. On the way to the crisis area, the *LA* participated in the first launch of a tactical Regulus I missile off Hawaiian waters. The missile's warhead was a reserve weapon with a depleted uranium core. Two F9F–6P's flying from NAS Barber's Point picked up the missile and guided it to a terminal dive at Kaula Rock off of Kauai Island. Nearing the target, one of the pilots armed the missile and guided it down for a high speed run to the target. Though the warhead detonated 300 yards short of the target due to air turbulence, the operation suitability test (OST) was a clear success. While it could be argued that this test was only a feasibility trial and not one of tactical availability, the deployment of an American cruiser armed with three nuclear missiles and an updated Trounce guidance system was unprecedented and historic. This system allowed the launching cruiser to control the missile for 350 miles and then hand off guidance to a second ship closer to the target. (18) Whether it was the Navy's presence in the area with tactical nuclear weapons, the well–coordinated evacuation of the Tachens, or both, the Chinese communists ended the shelling of Quemoy and Matsu Island in May.

When the crisis in the Formosa Straits receded, *the USS Los Angeles* began visiting friendly ports along the Pacific rim. Euphemistically called "Good will" calls by the Navy, over 25,000 sailors went ashore daily somewhere in Westpac. According to one observer, "They left behind a lot of friends," but they also left behind a lot of money, especially whenever they arrived just after pay day. (19) Yokosuka, Japan, continued to be a popular and convenient place for sailors. At times as many as 25,000 sailors, fresh from patrols, made the environs of the former Imperial Japanese Naval base into a steamy, artificially lit wonderland from noon to midnight. Yoko, as it was called by many, in time turned out to be a Japanese version of Las Vegas with a garish, mile–long strip. Dollars, converted into yen, flowed in the millions into Yoko and throughout the entire Japanese economy. (20)

During the spring of 1955 the *Los Angeles* made three notable "good will" port calls to friendly nations in the region. Potential enemy states were put on notice that the United States Navy in Asian waters was willing and able to intervene in local conflicts, strategically located. Friendly countries were aggressively wooed by these same naval forces. Friendly port visits by free–spending sailors were definitely part of the Navy's "people to people" program. Captain J. W. Waterhouse, CO of the *Los Angeles* in the spring of 1955, reminded his officers and men to, "Keep [up] your excellent 'diplomatic' record" as they left the ship for liberty.

The *LA's* visit to Cebu City in the Philippines from March 25–29, 1955, is a case in point. Located about 400 miles southeast of Manila, the port had rarely been visited by ships of the United States Navy. For this reason, careful preparations were made to insure a successful visit. Informational pamphlets were studied, and well–thought–out plans were made. Local representatives of the U.S. Information Service stationed in Cebu City made preparations for the port call, working with local officials.

According to an official report of the visit, the local response to the visit of the *USS Los Angeles* was excellent. (21) Cars, buses and army trucks were made available to take Americans from the landing to prearranged dances and athletic events. City police working with the shore patrol furnished a jeep for roving patrols. The city seemed honored to receive an American "capital" ship, not seen since the end of World War II.

Separate dances for officers and enlisted men were arranged, and congeniality was enhanced by the number of Filipinos who spoke English. But the biggest single "friendship factor" in the visit was the athletic competition between the *LA's* teams and local ones. Crowds of over 500 watched two baseball games and a basketball game between the ship's team and young Filipinos. The presence of the Commander Cruiser Division Five (ComCruDiv 5) band at the first game added to the excitement and enthusiasm of that event.

The ship's company responded warmly to the town's demonstration of good will. Seventy–five pints of blood were collected from shipboard volunteers and sent to a local blood bank. In another opportunity to show gratitude and thanks for Cebu City's reception, Americans pulled a native outrigger to safety when it got caught in a rain squall. In another response to the hospitality of the City of Cebu, the Commander of Cruiser Division Five (ComCruDiv 5) RADM F.B. Warder and the Commanding Officer of the USS *Los Angeles* Captain J.W. Waterhouse invited 300 guests to a reception on board the cruiser. After passing through a receiving line, the guests were taken on a tour of the ship and were shown an aerial display by the ship's helicopter. Boy Scouts and Cub Scouts as well came aboard to tour the ship.

The only negative factor in this port call was the high rate of VD in the town; ten cases of gonorrhea were contracted during the three days of liberty. Despite this lamentable occurrence, "It was generally felt that Cebu was a good liberty port, a place off the usual route, and thus more attractive." It was believed that, "A return trip would be worthwhile." (22)

A visit to the larger city of Kobe, Japan, on April 9, 1955, was a much different experience. The city had more recreational activities and shopping opportunities than the small town in the Philippines. Moreover by train Kobe was an hour away from the historic city of Kyoto and less than an hour away from Osaka. It was recommended that a tourist map of Kyoto, Osaka, Nava and Kobe be purchased, but the two–day stay in port was not enough time to visit many of the attractions in the area, and sailors were told to keep the maps for a return trip.

The crew heard a message from the *LA's* Commanding Officer as the ship tied up alongside a pier. This was the first time in a month everyone aboard could enjoy this "luxury." He announced to his officers and men the purpose of the ship's visit to Kobe. First of all, he said that they were to embark a Marine Naval Gunfire team in Kobe in preparation for fire support exercises off Okinawa the following week. Secondly, the visit would allow "liberty over the Easter holiday." Finally he told the men of the *Los Angeles* that the ship's real purpose for being in Kobe was to show the people of the city "that the United States Navy stands manned and ready" for any emergency in opposing "communist aggression." (23) The ship bulletin provided "Two Timely Tips" to liberty–bound sailors. The first "tip" described areas in the city that were out of bounds because of reported attacks on Americans. Another tip warned sailors about the prevalence of venereal disease in Kobe and admonished them to stay clear of prostitutes because, "Kobe prostitutes are among the sickest in Japan." Behavior ashore was said to be exemplary. The exception was the behavior of two Marines who were charged with larceny when they tried to steal a radio in a house of prostitution. (24)

The *USS Los Angeles* visited Toyama, Japan, on May 2, 1955, and departed on May 5. This was for a "good will" visit to a small city about one hundred miles northwest of Tokyo. Though the people were friendly and hospitable, the city proved to be a less attractive liberty port than the better known cities in Japan. For one thing there was an acute language barrier due to the city's isolation and the absence of any US military installations nearby. Entertainment and recreation facilities were limited by the rural character and the small size of the city. Liberty parties were small in number because during the visit, sea swells and high winds cancelled all small boating activity except for landing craft from the accompanying *USS Skagit* (AKA-105). As a result, VD casualties could not be evaluated because contacts were relatively few. (25)

Nonetheless there were many "people to people" events during the ship's stay. The *LA's* baseball team played the evenly matched Toyama City Team before 4,000 spectators. On the day of arrival, the ComCruDiv 5 band played a well–received concert at the city auditorium. Dinner parties and luncheons were given for small numbers of American officers in Toyama and two of the smaller towns nearby. In return the Cruiser Division Commander and the *LA's* C.O. entertained about fifty

Japanese officials and their wives at a shipboard reception. That evening, 14 of these officials were guests for dinner on board. (26)

After a seven–month tour with the 7th Fleet in Westpac, the *Los Angeles* and two other cruisers returned to Long Beach. Following the unloading of ammunition at the nearby Seal Beach Weapons Station, the cruisers emerged from the fog and entered Long Beach Harbor, and the *LA's* band played Dixieland, marches and ballroom ballads while docking. (27)

On October 23, 1955, RADM George C. Wright assumed command of Cruiser Division Five. Wright had been Director of the Atomic Energy division in the Chief of Naval Operations office. His new flag ship was the lead vessel in the Regulus I surface ship program. In late 1956, Captain Frederic C. Lucas, a three–time winner of the Navy Cross, became the Commanding Officer of the *USS Los Angeles* in a ceremony in Long Beach. Lucas became the sixth skipper of the ship since its recommissioning five years before.

In the late spring of 1956, the *Los Angeles* left Long Beach for another tour with the 7th Fleet. At this time President Eisenhower was reevaluating American containment and deterrent policies in the light of the French withdrawal from Indochina. A firm believer in the "domino theory," Eisenhower believed that country after country would fall to communism if the West surrendered to any one act of aggression in the Pacific Rim. He drew a line across the former French Indochina by supporting the South Vietnamese government of Ngo Diem, a fervent anticommunist. While substituting the South East Asia Treaty Organization (SEATO) for the hated legacy of the French domination, the president approved military and economic aid programs for Diem's government. Eisenhower, however, opposed any direct involvement in the impending Indochinese struggle. Any military adventure in the former French colony without allies was politically out of the question for the president. (28) Diem did not make the situation in South Vietnam easier for American policy makers. His refusal to allow free elections and the suppression of his political opposition allowed the communists a chance to seize power later.

Diem sought even closer ties with the United States as the war against the communists in South Vietnam developed. Impressed with the power of the U.S. Navy in the region, he asked for U.S. military participation in the celebration of South Vietnam's first Independence Day observance on October 26, 1956. Both the Commander–in–Chief of the Pacific Fleet (CINCPAC) Admiral Felix Stump and Chief of Naval Operations (CNO) Admiral Arleigh A. Burke endorsed the request. It was believed an Independence Day fly–over by planes from the *USS Essex* (CV–9) would favorably impress the South Vietnamese population. The *USS Los Angeles* (CA–135) was sent up the Saigon River to the capital for a four–day visit, celebrating the first anniversary of the Republic of South Vietnam. This visit to Saigon between October 24–28, 1956, was a carefully planned and well–studied operation. For example, along with a whole array of materials concerning South Vietnam, the 1954 visit to Saigon by the *USS Rochester* (CA–124) was carefully examined. In approaching the capital, the *USS Los Angeles* "was

President Ngo Dinh Diem , reviewing the USS Los Angeles *in the Saigon River at Saigon, South Vietnam, on the first anniversary of the Republic of Vietnam, October 26, 1959.* U.S. NAVY

turned in the Saigon River northeast of the city by dropping her starboard anchor underfoot." In a maneuver which put the bow against the bank, the ship's engines were twisted and, with the assistance of tugs, the cruiser was able to back clear" as it moved up the river. (29) The river trip to Saigon was 46 miles with narrow stretches and sharp bends along the way.

Because of the diplomatic importance of this port call, the 15–piece band from Carrier Division One was put at the disposal of the Commanding Officer of the *Los Angeles*. It was also recommended that dock and ship sentries be maintained in this very volatile area. (30)

Upon entering the harbor, the *Los Angeles* fired a 21–gun salute, followed by a reply from the Bach Dang battery nearby. A Vietnamese band then played the American national anthem. The next day RADM Wright and Captain Lucas signed President Diem's Gold Book in the Independence Palace. When an eager crowd stormed the pier at the beginning of general visiting hours, ship's personnel and not local police controlled the visitors by having them form a line two abreast for boarding. (31)

On Friday, October 26, RADM Wright, Captain Lucas and six ship's officers viewed a parade of units of the South Vietnamese armed forces. Later that day Diem visited all naval forces in the harbor. As the President of South Vietnam reviewed the *Los Angeles* in his motor launch, a Regulus I missile was in clear sight. The *Los Angeles* rendered the president a full 21–gun salute as his launch approached the heavy cruiser. President Diem was also honored on October 27 with a formal dinner aboard ship.

For enlisted men Saigon was a very expensive city. Hotels and restaurants with French names had the aura of Paris. Night clubs were in abundance, but the price tag was high and the entertainment mediocre. It was therefore recommended that overnight liberty in the city not be granted. Recreational activities available were to be found in an Enlisted Men's Club, movie theaters that showed American movies, at the USIA library, at sports events and on tours. (32) Sailors had to acclimate themselves to the siesta periods from 1200 to 1500 daily.

The visit to the new Republic of South Vietnam by an American man–of–war provided both evidence of American armed strength and America's interest in that southeast Asian country. However, the American naval attache to South Vietnam cautioned higher authorities about the developing political realities in the new republic. He believed that the visit of powerful warships and planes might give the South Vietnamese people the impression that Americans were trying to replace the French as the new colonial masters in the region. In any event, RADM Wright repeated the naval attache's concerns in a report to his superiors in the 7th Fleet. He wrote that visits to Saigon "not be made too frequently in order to avoid creating any impression that the United States is moving in to replace the French domination over the Vietnamese." (33)

By 1957 the presence of the 7th Fleet along the Asian littoral became normal routine once again. Between tracking submarines and destroyers, the fleet kept a constant watch on Chinese communist coastal traffic. Destroyers conscientiously patrolled the Formosa Straits. On liberty, sailors feasted on the delights of such ports as Hong Kong, Singapore and Manila. Vice Admiral Wallace Beakley, commander of the 7th Fleet and a man of recognized diplomatic skills, stated, "We have to fly the flag for our friends to see, but we must not show it too often. Our friends must see the flag often enough to be reassured that we are here." (34) This remark was testimony to the fact he was well grounded in the colonial history of the region.

After a three–year hiatus, the simmering Formosa Straits problem exploded once again into a serious crisis on August 23, 1958. Chinese communist guns began shelling the offshore island of Quemoy with a bombardment reminiscent of the savagery of Verdun in World War I. American planners were hard pressed to know whether or not this action presaged an invasion of the islands and if it did, was it a prelude to an eventual invasion of Taiwan. Any American commitment to Quemoy remained ambiguous, while Taiwan's security was guaranteed, but Admiral Arleigh A. Burke, the Chief of Naval Operations, believed that the loss of the offshore islands would, at the very least, constitute a loss of prestige for the United States in the region. With concurrent tensions in Lebanon unraveling and American forces spread thinly around the world, there was some thought of using tactical nuclear weapons against the Chinese. Burke had the authority at that time to reinforce American naval units in the troubled Formosa Straits. He did just that, and the Administration agreed. The USS Essex (CV–9) was dispatched quickly from the Mediterranean, and the USS Los Angeles and the USS Midway (CV–41) were ordered from their west coast ports to Formosan waters. The 7th Fleet now had six aircraft carriers and a total of 50 ships. Yet, according to the New York Times, the U.S. officials who were instrumental in moving the ships speedily to the Orient indicated that the ship movements were precautionary and "taken only for safety's sake." (35) President Eisenhower had mixed feelings about the use of tactical nuclear weapons and wanted to avoid military action. He therefore opted for a policy of passive assistance to the nationalists on the offshore islands. He ordered the U.S. Navy to help bring in supplies to the 100,000 nationalist troops on the besieged island. (36)

The night the Los Angeles received orders to rush to the Far East had been a busy and hectic one. Earlier that day, the cruiser had been conducting gunnery exercises off the coast of California when quite a different message had been received. A fishing boat near San Nicholas Island was taking on water and sinking. The Los Angeles was the first ship on the scene. At 2400 engineers boarded the disabled boat and in five minutes got the boat's pumps working again. An hour later, the fishing craft was on its way home. It was while steaming back to Long Beach that the tired crew heard the call for immediate assistance in the Far East. The Operations Officer announced that Quemoy was under fire and an invasion of that island was imminent. The cruiser was ordered to leave for the Far East at 0800 that very morning! The departure, however, was delayed 24 hours so that three fleet training missiles the cruiser had on board could be exchanged for three tactical missiles armed with W–27 thermonuclear warheads. The LA finally left port for the western Pacific the next day, racing toward Hawaii at 27 knots. After a short layover, the ship headed for the

Formosa Straits to join Task Force 72–2. A cruise book writer on the LA later described the ships's actions as an example of "flexibility, mobility and versatility in action." (37)

By the time the LA had arrived in the Formosa Straits, the crisis had cooled down, but on October 4 the cruiser took up a position as an aircraft control ship 14 miles off Quemoy. There the LA tracked Chinese communist planes while supporting one of the largest American supply efforts in the Far East. Two Chinese nationalist officers boarded the cruiser as air controllers for their aircraft. (38) Gun crews on the cruiser remained at general quarters, ready to fire back if hostile planes seemed to be maneuvering for an attack. Several communist jets flew just a few miles from the LA but always turned back. The Los Angeles and other American warships stood fast until the Chinese communists began to lessen their barrage on the offshore island. During the sea–lift, the Chinese communists did not to fire on American warships, and some of them moved to safer places to avoid an incident. Though nationalist supply ships

The USS Los Angeles *honors American war dead off Midway Island, April 27, 1959.* U.S. NAVY

were fired upon, the sea–lift to Quemoy succeeded. The *Los Angeles'* Public Information officer Ensign Joseph C. Walker told reporters later that there had been some real "scares" for the men of the *LA* in this "eyeball to eyeball" confrontation. (39)

There were several reasons why the United States may have decided not to use nuclear weapons when it appeared that a clash was evident. First of all, the Chinese were careful to not to fire on or sink American ships convoying supplies to the besieged island. This restraint may have been due to the fact that they were unclear as to whether Eisenhower would use nuclear weapons or not. The Chinese were probably aware that as NATO commander, the American president had been quoted as saying that he would use nuclear weapons "instantly...[if the] net advantage of their use was on my [our] side." But Eisenhower valued his European alliances, and understood what effect nuclear strikes or even the bombing of the mainland would have on American diplomacy. Unknown to the Chinese was Secretary of State John Foster Dulles' retreat from the notion of massive retaliation after he was told by the Atomic Energy Commission (AEC) that a nuclear strike on the Chinese mainland would kill eight million Chinese. (40) For unknown reasons, the Chinese communists eased the assault on Quemoy by bombarding the island every other day. A cease fire followed on October 5, lasting until this day. In 1974 CINCPAC Admiral Harry Felt recalled:

> *It is true that at the time (in the 1958 crisis) we had plans for the use of tactical nuclear weapons. Most of us believed in those days that the use of tactical nuclear weapons wouldn't key off the big war, and we didn't have any plan to do it any other way.* (41)

The possibility that the United States might use nuclear weapons, plus the presence of a powerful American fleet in the Formosa Straits probably explain why the Chinese backed down again over Quemoy. Those reasons for this retreat were reinforced by the fact that nationalist troops on the island were being successfully resupplied by sea.

At this juncture, the *Los Angeles* moved south with Task Force 77.2 for a few days, then entered Kaoshiung, Taiwan, for rest and relaxation. Shortly afterwards the crew of the *Los Angeles* heard about a typhoon which had devastated a Japanese village. The ship's crew voluntarily contributed $1,142 for relief. This contribution was the largest donation given by any ship in the 7th Fleet. After visiting ports such as Buckner Bay in Okinawa, Yokosuka and Yokohama in Japan, and Pearl Harbor, the *Los Angeles* arrived back at its home port of Long beach on December 5, in time to celebrate the Christmas season. (42)

The cruiser *Los Angeles* sailed periodically with the 7th Fleet until she was retired on November 15, 1963. The time between the Quemoy–Matsu crisis of 1958 and the Vietnam war was a time of relative calm in the western Pacific. The 7th Fleet, however, still maintained a balanced fleet of 125 ships and 60,000 men in the area. The fleet included three attack aircraft carriers, an antisubmarine and helicopter carrier and a surface patrol force consisting of three cruisers, several destroyer squadrons and a submarine force. This fleet patrolled an area from 600 miles east of Guam to the middle of the Indian Ocean and from the Arctic to the Antarctic, one fifth of the world's surface. Patrols along the Formosa Straits were made daily, mainly by destroyers. The fleet's tasks continued to include "goodwill" visits to friendly ports and readiness exercises for limited or nuclear war. The American presence along the 3,500–mile diagonal of tension from Tokyo to Singapore had a diplomatic objective. The fleet stood ready to back American interests in the region, using either slight force or a lot of it. Ranged against the fleet were a total of 130 Soviet and Chinese Communist submarines, a growing Soviet Pacific fleet and a huge Chinese army on the mainland. By the late 1950s the Chinese communist air force was rated as the fourth largest in the world. (43)

In late November 1959, the U.S. Navy, the Navy League and the Treasury Department planned a "remembrance day" for the cruiser *Los Angeles,* commemorating the successful bond drive 16 years before. Los Angeles civic leaders and celebrities who had organized and spearheaded the Treasury Department's bond drive were invited to join the officers and men of the *Los Angeles* for a cruise on November 16, 1959. They witnessed a "sea battle" off Long Beach with Navy planes, helicopters, a destroyer, a submarine and the *Los Angeles* demonstrating what one newspaper editorial described as, "Effective sea power." It was hoped that those on board and the public at large, also invited to visit the ship in Long Beach, might "learn about sea power in the atomic age." The public was urged to note the *LA's* "new role as a man–of–war, capable of firing guided missiles." The Navy and the Navy League were anxious to show that these were the "ultimate weapons to guarantee peace" because there was no reliable way of locating these "missile platforms" at sea. The Treasury Department's involvement in this program was to promote their case for raising money for research

A four–man U.S. Marine color guard from the heavy cruiser Los Angeles, *participating in the opening ceremonies at the Los Angeles Coliseum during the World Series, October 8, 1959.* U.S. NAVY

and weapons development to keep the peace. Their slogan was "peace power [is made] by sale of savings bonds." (44)

On August 11, 1961, the *Los Angeles* left Long Beach for another deployment with the 7th Fleet and met 12 ships to form the largest group of ships to sail together since World War II. Among them was the carrier *USS Ranger* (CVA–61) and later the carrier *USS Yorktown* (CV–10). As the permanent flagship of Commander Cruiser Division One (ComCruDiv 1), the *LA* had tactical command of this unit. The ships were on regular rotational assignment and were not responding to any emergency. The *LA* arrived at Sasebo, Japan, and relieved the cruiser *USS Topeka* (CLG–8).

The "people to people" program of the Eisenhower administration was continued by President Kennedy. It was believed that the program was "creating an enormous amount of good will" in the Far East. The men of the *Los Angeles* toured Beppi, Japan, and had a reception there. They visited orphanages in Kobe, Osaka and Kyoto and presented the children with toys. In a four–day visit to Kagashima, they brought that city's destitute population food and clothing. In a ceremony in that southern Japanese town, Rear Admiral E.A. Ruckner, Commander of Cruiser Division One (ComCruDiv 1), laid a wreath at the tomb of Japanese naval hero Heihachiro Togo. These kinds of activities strengthened the bond of friendship between the two countries, making American sailors welcome in many quarters.

The *LA* then sailed to Yokosuka where sailors on liberty could take a train to Tokyo. Christmas was spent in Hong Kong. One of the activities in that British Crown Colony was a party for underprivileged children. After a cruise to the Philippines, the *LA* arrived back in Long Beach in late February. The deployment had covered 42,000 nautical miles. (45)

The *USS Los Angeles'* last cruise to the Far East took place in 1962 and 1963. Leaving in November 1962, the Cruise Book of that year restated what was believed to be the mission of the ship as she steamed west. It read, "We represent our country as the true preserver of the inalienable rights which Communism would usurp." Tensions with communist China continued to shape American diplomatic and military policy in the

Far East. The 14 ports in Japan, Korea, Okinawa, Taiwan, Hong Kong and the Philippine Islands also had problems with mainland China. Among the more interesting visits was a stopover in Shimoda, Japan, where the Black Ship Festival was being celebrated. This Festival commemorates the opening of Japan to the West by Commodore Mathew C. Perry. Perry had sailed for Japan in 1853 to obtain coaling stations and trade guarantees for Americans. The opening of trade with Japan was the key provision of the Treaty of Kanagawa, signed in 1854. The name "Black Ship" derived from Perry's coal–burning ships which bellowed black smoke that seemed so strange to the people of this small, seaside town less than a hundred miles from Yokosuka. The highlight of the festival was the reenactment of meeting between men dressed in Samurai costumes who acted as representatives of Shogun Tokugawa and those dressed as

Perry and his sailors. A string of other activities took place in conjunction with this event. The closeness of Mount Fuji to Shimoda made this Japanese national symbol accessible to the visitors.

In summary, the eight deployments of the cruiser *USS Los Angeles* (CA–135) to the western Pacific (WestPac) served the needs and interests of American diplomacy. The mission of the 7th Fleet in the region was twofold: to maintain stability in an area menaced by communist expansion and anticolonial revolts and to promote good will vital to the growth of the American economy. This last cruise was a typical peace time cruise, keeping alive one of the 7th Fleet's slogans, "We have no schedule and we adhere to it." (46) The situation in Viet Nam had not as yet arisen to test the maintenance of this status quo.

The commissary crew of the USS Los Angeles, *setting up service for a steak dinner, March 24, 1958.* U.S. NAVY

Showing visiting wives the ship's electronic systems, June 30, 1958. U.S. NAVY

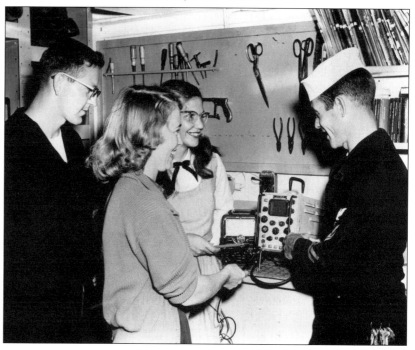

END NOTES

(1)   *Long Beach Press–Telegram,* June 14, 1954.

(2)   A.M. Rosenthal, "On Patrol with the Seventh Fleet," *New York Times Magazine,* October 1, 1961, pp. 27–82–83.

(3)   Malcolm Muir, Jr., *Black Shoes and Blue Water: Surface Warfare in the United States Navy, 1945–1975* (Washington: Naval Historical Center, 1996), p. 35.

(4)   *Los Angeles Examiner,* July 21, 1954.

(5)   David K. Stumpf, *Regulus: The Forgotten Weapon* (Paducah: Turner Publishing Co., 1996) p. 95.

(6)   Muir, op. cit., p. 51.

(7)   *Ibid.,* p. 83.

(8)   Stumpf, op. cit., p. 61.

(9)   Muir, op. cit., p. 92.

(10)   Quoted in Muir, *ibid.,* p. 93.

(11)   *Ibid.,* p. 93.

(12)   *Ibid.*

(13)   *Long Beach Press–Telegram*, May 11, 1958; *San Pedro News–Pilot*, May 12, 1958.

(14)   Muir, op. cit., p. 94.

(15)   *Ibid.,* p. 95; Elmo Zumwalt, *On Watch: A Memoir* (New York:, Quadrangle, 1976), p. 81.

(16)   Michael T. Eisenberg, *Shield of the Republic: The United States Navy in an Era of Cold War and Violent Peace, 1945–1962,* Vol. I (New York: St. Martin's Press), p. 619.

(17)   *Long Beach Press–Telegram,* February 8, 1955.

(18)   Stumpf, op. cit., p. 86. Muir, op. cit., p. 51.

(19)   Eisenberg, op. cit., p. 624.

(20)   *Ibid.,* p. 604

(21)   "Visit to Cebu City, Republic of the Philippines," A4–5, Ser. 535, 9 April 1955, p. 2.

(22)   *Ibid.,* p. 3.

(23)   "Visit to Kobe Japan," A4–5, Ser. 595, 16 April, 1955, Enclosure (1).

(24)   *Ibid.,* p. 2.

(25)   "Visit to Toyoma, Japan," 2–4 May 1955, A4–5 , Ser. 161, 24 May 1955, p. 3.

(26)   *Ibid.*

(27   *Long Beach Press–Telegram,* August 22, 1955.

(28)   Robert Divine, *Eisenhower and the Cold War,* (New York: Oxford University Press), 1981 pp. 52–54.

(29)   "Visit to Saigon, 24-28 October 1956, A4-5, Ser 1734, 9 November 1956, p. 2.

(30)   Office of Naval Attache, Saigon, Viet Nam, "General Information," Enclosure (1) Part 1, p. 2.

(31)   "Visit to Saigon," op. cit., p. 2.

(32) Office of Naval Attache, op. cit., p. 5.

(33) ComCruDiv 5 to Com SEVENTH FLEET, "Report of Visit to Saigon, Vietnam, 24–28 October 1956," A4–5, Ser. 480, 23 November 1956; Edward B. Hooper, Dean C. Allard and Oscar P. Fitzgerald, *The United States Navy and the Viet Nam Conflict, Vol. I: The Setting of the Stage to 1959,* (Washington: Naval History Division, Department of the Navy, 1976), p. 341.

(34) Quoted in Eisenberg, op. cit., p. 622.

(35) *New York Times,* August 29, 1958.

(36) Stephen Howarth, *To Shining Sea: A History of the United States Navy, 1775–1991* (New York: Random House, 1991), p. 500.

(37) Cruise Book, *USS Los Angeles,* 1958–59, p. 20.

(38) Stumpf, op. cit., p. 100.

(39) *Long Beach Press–Telegram,* December 5, 1958.

(40) Walter Pincus, "In the 40s and 50s Nuclear Arms Still Seemed Usable," *Washington Post,* July 22, 1985.

(41) Quoted in Peter Hayes, Lyuba Zarsky and Walden Bellow, *American Lake: Nuclear Peril in the Pacific* (New York: Penguin Books, 1986), p. 57.

(42) Cruise Book, op. cit., p. 36.

(43) William H. Hessler, "The Seventh Fleet is Ready," *Reporter,* June 8, 1961. pp. 30–31.

(44) *Long Beach Press–Telegram,* November 12, 1959; *San Pedro News–Pilot,* November 12, 1959.

(45) *Long Beach Press–Telegram,* February 25, 1962.

(46) Cruise Book, *USS Los Angeles,* 1962–63, pp. 126–28.

TO THE SCRAPYARD

By the late 1950s Chief of Naval Operations (CNO) Arleigh Burke realized that air defense had to improve if the fleet was to meet the challenges of enhanced Soviet air capabilities. In 1957 Congress appropriated money for nine missile cruisers for this purpose. Many of these ships would not be new ships but converted World War II–era cruisers. Six *Cleveland*–class light cruisers and three *Baltimore*–class heavy cruisers went to the yards for extensive overhauls. All the other gun ships of the *Baltimore*–class, even those with Regulus I land attack missile launchers like the *USS Los Angeles,* were to be phased out, with the exception of the *USS St. Paul* (CA–73). Two of the newly converted missile ships, the *USS Chicago* (CG–11) and the *USS Columbus* (CG–12), were sister ships of the *Los Angeles.* They were completely reconstructed with a modern appearance due to their so-called "MACKS," a combination of Masts and stacks sensors and missiles from stem to stern. The *Columbus* (CG–12) was commissioned in 1962, the *Chicago* (CG–10) in 1964. Guns were removed from these ships and twin Talos launchers were placed forward and aft. Twin Tartar launchers were also placed on each side of their bridge structures. Also entering the fleet in the 1960s were 18 new missile–cruisers of the *Leahy*– and *Belknap*–class, plus several large, nuclear–powered cruisers as well. (1)

It was determined, therefore, that the *USS Los Angeles* and other older cruisers would be retired from service to make way for the flood of new ships entering service. In a ceremony on November 15,1963, at the Long Beach Naval Station, the Commanding Officer of the *Los Angeles* Commander Philip H. Klepak ordered the national ensign hauled down, signaling the beginning of the retirement of the venerable warship. Her new home would be the Pacific Reserve Fleet in San Diego where she would once again join the "mothball" fleet. A speech by Rear Admiral William H. Groverman, Commander Cruiser–Destroyer Flotilla Three, was the highlight of this solemn retirement ceremony. The Admiral finished his talk by noting, "A ship like the *Los Angeles* will never die, nor fade away, but live on forever in our hearts and in our country's history." (2)

An announcement almost a decade later that the cruiser *Los Angeles* was going to be scrapped offered warship enthusiasts and local citizens alike the prospect of saving the ship as a permanent memorial in Los Angeles Harbor. It was believed that public support could be generated by linking the preservation of the ship with the patriotic sentiment engendered by a nation celebrating its Bicentennial Year in 1976. In early April 1974, the American Society of Military History (ASMH), a nonprofit organization, began looking for a permanent berth for the *USS Los Angeles* as part of the Bicentennial celebration. The General Manager of the Harbor Department also began studying the problem of berthing the ship, but he was hesitant because of the lack of visitor parking. (3) A call for more funds from the public was not heeded, thus hurting the entire cause. Nineteen–seventy–six was still far off, and many believed it was always hard to motivate people for an event so far in the future, but not much money was donated even as the event came closer. Disappointed as the scrapping of the warship seemed more likely, County Supervisor Kenneth Hahn, a former naval officer, wrote the Assistant Secretary of the Navy in the spring of 1975 about local efforts to save the ship. The Secretary's reply was anything but encouraging. He wrote Hahn that ASMH had shortcomings and lacked "any firm long range plan for the ship memorial." Moreover there were still unanswered questions about a mooring site and maintenance funds. (4) On the other hand, a spokesman for the ASMH, based in South El Monte, California, said that the effort to preserve and display the *USS Los Angeles* in Los Angeles Harbor collapsed because the Los Angeles Harbor Department did not provide the required dock space at a reasonable price. Moreover he indicated that the main person in the Harbor Department was not sympathetic to military projects in the harbor. (5) Though Hahn said he would continue to fight for the preservation of the ship, the cruiser's fate was already sealed. As one local newspaper noted, "No luck, no money—and now the end is near." (6) The absence of interest and therefore of money donated for the project may have been due in part to the current antimilitary mood in the country. Some might call it a manifestation of the "Vietnam War Syndrome." This was the time when the war in Vietnam was coming to an unpleasant end. The American people watched on TV the helicopters from 7th Fleet ships evacuating Americans from rooftops in Saigon as the communists were poised to enter the city. (7)

The *USS Los Angeles* (CA–135) was doomed. The U.S. Navy would receive an estimated one million dollars from the breakers. On June 12, 1974, the cruiser arrived in San Pedro's Main Channel after a 20–hour tow from San Diego. It must have been sad for anyone who knew the ship's history to see her unpainted and rusty silhouette move slowly up San Pedro's main channel. After all, she was once the "glamour girl" of the fleet, and more importantly, the recipient of five battle stars for two combat tours during the Korean War. As tugs headed her toward the breaking yard in the east channel, one observer said, "She came home to die in a scrap heap." (8)

Mindful of community sentiment, the salvage operators promised to save the ship's bell for display in San Pedro. On an earlier occasion, another ship's bell from the *USS Los Angeles* had been loaned to the Cabrillo Marine Museum in San Pedro in late 1960. At that time the cruiser was undergoing a mod-

ernization refit which called for more space. The 1,200–pound bell simply needed a smaller replacement. Rather than scrapping it, the Navy gave the bell to the city of Los Angeles on an "indefinite loan." (9) The second bell was given to the City as well.

While the ship was being scrapped, there were those who sought to retain some of the ships' memorabilia in order to commemorate the gallant ship's service. Acceding to the joint request of City Councilman John S. Gibson Jr. (Fifteenth District) and the Mayor of Los Angeles Tom Bradley, Joseph Shapiro, President of the National Metal and Steel Company, in a gesture to the Bicentennial Celebration, donated the mast of the *Los Angeles* to the city. I. Roy Coates, the company's Salvage Officer, saved much of the ship's memorabilia.

The effort to bring a suitable memorial for the ship in San Pedro became a joint community endeavor. The ten–ton, 93–foot main mast of the cruiser *Los Angeles* became the centerpiece of a memorial at John Gibson Park, adjacent to the Los Angeles Maritime Museum on San Pedro's main channel. The mast has the same 6-degree angle as it had when it towered above the cruiser's deck. The Red Stack Tugboat Company provided a tug and a barge to move the mast across the channel. The Crescent Wharf and Warehouse Company donated a crane to lift the mast to the ground where it would be sandblasted and painted. Pacific Outdoor Advertising Co. assisted by moving the mast to the park. Coordinated Equipment Co. of Wilmington donated the rigging of the cable stays, once the mast was in place. (10) The San Pedro Historical Society offered its help cataloging photographs and news clippings.

The Ship Mast Monument was dedicated at the John Gibson Jr. Park on December 1, 1977. Along with the mast are two bow anchors, on permanent loan from the Navy. They will be erected on a concrete foundation at the park. The memorial honors the men who lost their lives in the naval service. A military–style ceremony was led by Councilman John S. Gibson of Los Angeles and Rear Admiral Frank Higbee, Ret. CG. They led a mast–stepping ceremony in which coins were placed under the mast, a maritime gesture of good luck. (11)

Other items on display commemorating the *USS Los Angeles* placed in and around the Los Angeles Maritime Museum include a bow section, a flying bridge, the ship's bell, steering wheel, engine room telegraph and compass binnacle. Also on exhibit in the Museum are large models of the cruiser *USS Los Angeles* (CA–135), the naval airship *USS Los Angeles* (ZR–3) and the nuclear attack submarine *USS Los Angeles* (SSN–688). Along with pictures and posters on display in the Museum's Navy room is a 6x15–foot oil painting by illustrator Duncan Gleason, depicting the heavy cruiser. (12)

On October 6, 1995, the 50th anniversary of the heavy cruiser's first commissioning in 1945 was marked by a public ceremony in which Rudy Svorinich Jr., a Los Angeles City Councilman, spoke at John S. Gibson Jr. Park on behalf of the people of the harbor area. Finally, in tribute to the memory of the ship, the *USS Los Angeles* (CA–135) Association had its reunion in the Los Angeles area that same year. (13)

END NOTES

(1)   Malcom Muir, Jr. *Black Shoes and Blue Water: Surface warfare in the United States Navy, 1945-1975* (Washington: Naval Historical Center, 1996), p. 84; Captain John Moore, RN, Editor, *Jane's Fighting Ships, 1977-78* (New York: Franklin Watts, Inc., 1977, pp. 582–59.

(2)   *San Pedro News–Pilot,* November 15, 1963.

(3)   *Long Beach Press–Telegram,* April 2, 1974.

(4)   *Ibid.,* April 1, 1975.

(5)   Phone interview with Craig Michelson, May 5, 1999.

(6)   *Long Beach Independent,* June 1, 1975.

(7)   Norman Polmar, *Chronology of the Cold War* (Annapolis: Naval Institute Press, 1998), p. 157.

(8)   *Long Beach Press–Telegram,* June 12, 1975.

(9)   *Los Angeles Examiner,* December 16, 1960.

(10) City of Los Angeles, *Fact Sheet on the* USS Los Angeles *Navy Monument*, October 20, 1977.

(11) *San Pedro News–Pilot,* December 1, 1977; *Fact Sheet, ibid.*

(12) *Fact Sheet, ibid.; Long Beach Press–Telegram,* December 2, 1979.

(13) *San Pedro News–Pilot,* October 6, 1995.

Truck moving ship's main mast to John Gibson Park, San Pedro, California, 1977.
SAN PEDRO BAY HISTORICAL SOCIETY